Eero Saarinen

Eero Saarinen
by Allan Temko

George Braziller New York

To my Mother and Father

*To honor Eero Saarinen, Fellow of the American
Institute of Architects and recipient of its Gold
Medal, the College of Fellows of the American
Institute of Architects is pleased to sponsor this book.*

For information address the publisher,
George Braziller, Inc.
One Park Avenue
New York, New York 10016
Library of Congress Catalog Card Number: 62–16266
Printed in the United States of America
Second Printing

Contents

To have been born crown prince in a small, mildly old-fashioned, but humane and personal realm of architecture, over which his father Eliel ruled with firm benevolence—and then suddenly to have transformed that inheritance into a sweeping and powerful domain of his own, only to die tragically at the height of his powers—was Eero Saarinen's unique fate in the contemporary movement. No architect of the generation which followed the early Modernists enjoyed quite his particular advantages. None was more prodigiously equipped to profit from the lessons of the pioneers, including the deliberate teachings of his father, who groomed him from childhood to be a master.

Whether or not Eero Saarinen may be ranked as an authentic master of the modern age, on the order of Frank Lloyd Wright, Mies van der Rohe, or Le Corbusier, it is still too early to decide. For his career, surging forward amidst the diverse pressures of American life, was notably uneven; indeed, it was marred by misbegotten or hastily executed works which he later criticized with Tolstoyan earnestness. Not until the end of his life, when there were only a few choice commissions in the office at any time, and he had assembled one of the finest staffs in the world, did he display a steady efflorescence, developing an heroic sculptural architecture in concrete, and masterfully refining his objective and logical architecture in steel.

Consequently his ultimate significance in the Modern movement will depend not on celebrated—but comparatively weak—earlier works such as the General Motors Technical Center, but on the searching excellence of his final projects. Although these were fully designed at his death, they remain largely unfinished or scarcely begun. Yet because of the unprecedented spatial and structural expressions he was striving to achieve, these last creations must be experienced as three-dimensional realities in their actual surroundings, and further tested against the functional needs and spiritual aspirations of the age, before they may be conclusively appraised. There are few new buildings which demand such criteria, and this alone is a measure of their architect. The gap left by his death makes clear that none of his contemporaries who are presently in vogue in fact approached the boldness, depth, and heroic commitment of Saarinen's search

10 for new solutions to the problems of designing in a technological civilization.

Like all audacious searches, this one occasionally took a wrong turn to an impasse. Yet at the time of his death on September 1, 1961, shortly after his fifty-first birthday, the search seemed near fulfillment.

On the green plain of northern Virginia an incomparable airport (plate 103)—the first intended exclusively for jets, and also the first which promises to serve completely the rapidly changing requirements of a great air terminal—was under construction. Not only as a functional airport, however, but as a formal essay in concrete and as an expression of Federal character, this new gateway to Washington could be recognized as the crowning achievement of his career.

At the same time in New Jersey the immense rectilinear frame of Bell Laboratories' new research center was taking form—basically a Miesian form, but Saarinen's alone in its internal organization, and set in a resplendent baroque park which Saarinen alone could have conceived. Ultimately the structure would be cloaked in fastidiously detailed curtain walls of "mirror glass"—a new glass developed for the Saarinen office, and a typical example of the architect's inventive use of technology (plate 71).

And on the St. Louis riverfront the emplacement of the Jefferson Westward Expansion Memorial was also being prepared with sumptuous baroque energy, and the gigantic hoop of stainless steel—probably the most ambitious symbolic monument yet undertaken in the 20th century—at last was scheduled to rise beside the Mississippi, fourteen years after Saarinen had won the competition for its design (plates 133, 134).

Although the grand clarity of the original concept for the Jefferson arch ostensibly left little room for change, the design had nevertheless been meticulously reconsidered—and as I shall show, fundamentally improved—during the intervening years. Such perfectionism Eero Saarinen called "responsible architecture": architecture which takes full cognizance of the complex needs of site, structure, and program, and resolves them—logically but passionately—in a single, unified "expression."

This kind of responsibility transcends personal style when it is fully realized in terms of industrial technology: it belongs, as the finest architecture of the past inevitably did, to

a whole epoch. Yet the search for such an architecture was in
the profoundest sense an individual's quest for truth, and
came to Eero Saarinen as a birthright. For to the end, although he was always his own man, he was also the son of
Eliel Saarinen, who considered "spiritual function" inseparable from "practical function," and who described civilized
existence itself as a "search for form."

"Always think of the next larger thing."

ELIEL TO EERO SAARINEN

The steep-roofed studio house of granite and timber which 29-year-old Eliel Saarinen and his young architectural partners built in 1902—"Hvitträsk"—was named after the solemn, magnificent lake it overlooked from a wooded bluff eighteen miles from Helsinki. At a time when men such as Henri van de Velde had been so outraged by the *"mensonge des formes"* which falsified modern civilization, Eliel Saarinen had deserted the city for a sprawling, 38-room, rural retreat which, in spite of its romantic massing, picturesque detailing, and handicraft character was an essentially modern building in its thoughtful siting, functional plan, and veracious use of humble materials. It was also the furthest northern outpost of the highest European culture of the early 20th century. Here came Sibelius and Mahler, Gorki, the German critic Julius Meier-Graefe and the Swedish sculptor Carl Milles, who would later join Saarinen at Cranbrook in the United States. There was high talk and high fun: skating and boating on the lake, skiing on the hills, and parties which have become legendary.

Above all "Hvitträsk" was a wonderful place for children. In 1904 Eliel Saarinen married Loja Gesellius, his partner's sister, who was a gifted sculptor, weaver, photographer, a maker of architectural models, and, above all, a woman of heart. Their daughter Eva-Lisa, called Pipsan, was born the following year (after a long wedding trip which took them, among other places, to England for a study of railroad stations as part of Eliel's research for his monumental Helsinki terminal). Eero—the name is the Finnish form of Eric—was born five years later, on August 20, 1910. The boy was sensitive, thoughtful, and soft-spoken, as he would remain, but at the same time robustly energetic. He was also a prodigy who soon sketched precociously with either hand.

Very early the children were designing for themselves, drawing, painting, modeling beside their parents in the 90-foot studio-living room which was the center of the household (plates 1–3). The children's efforts were taken with the utmost seriousness by the entire family. Eliel liked to recall that he had received from his parents (his father was a

14 strongly dedicated Lutheran minister) "above all, a love for work." This in turn he imparted to Eero and Pipsan, together with that staunch moral resolution which the Finns call *sisu*, and which Eero later translated simply as "extended guts," a capacity to keep going even beyond the limits of energy and expected resources. *Sisu* precludes sentimentality, and emphasizes the need for deep personal commitment in any creative action. Each object, Eliel taught Pipsan and Eero, should be designed in its "next largest context—a chair in a room, a room in a house, a house in an environment, environment in a city plan."

In 1922, when he was twelve, Eero took first place in a Swedish matchstick design contest. At about the same time his father, an inveterate competitor, won the $20,000 second prize in the international competition for the Chicago *Tribune* Tower. The prize changed the course of the architect's life by bringing him to the United States. In April, 1923, Loja, Pipsan, and Eero joined Eliel in New York before they all moved on to the Midwest. Eero could not sleep his first night in Manhattan. "The traffic is all mixed up and wrong," he told his father in the morning. "It ought to be changed." He was not yet thirteen years old.

Preparation and Partnership
Two years later, in gently rolling country north of Detroit, the Saarinens were permanently at home in the United States. Until World War II they would return to Finland every summer; otherwise the move was final. Eero was always to consider himself an American architect; and although he retained a slight Finnish accent, he thought and acted as a man fully established in a new society. Yet in many respects their new home at Cranbrook, the unique school which they would all help to create over the next two decades (thanks to the philanthropies of the Detroit millionaire George C. Booth) was an enlarged, Americanized version of "Hvitträsk." It became a center of high culture and serious environmental thought in a part of the world where little of either had previously existed. Except for Wright's Taliesin, it was the only stopping place of its kind in the heartland of the United States.

In truth, there were few places in the world—the vastly more significant Bauhaus of course was one—where every

field of design, from textiles and metalwork to architecture
and city planning, was encompassed in so comprehensive a
curriculum.

If Cranbrook is pictorial architecture, tinged with historical reminiscence that led Wright to dismiss Eliel Saarinen
scornfully as "the best of the eclectics," these sensitively organized buildings and spaces—now that they have aged as
the architect intended—may be recognized as a superbly
ordered *total* environment. The remarkably consistent use of
fine materials, the unfailing control of scale, the play of
water, the integration of Carl Milles' sculpture with the
broad idealism of the concept, and above all the logical se-
quence of passages, courts, and monumental larger spaces,
coming one after the other in telling order, and tied together
by adroitly drawn pavements and stairs, all combine to make
a masterpiece of environmental planning. Even Eliel Saarinen's habitual reliance on strong vertical forms—towers and
chimneys—to contrast with spreading horizontal volumes
does not seem an arbitrary device, as in so much else of his
work, because of the rhythmic vitality of the whole (plate 4).

The whole family's creative powers were brought to bear
throughout the Cranbrook complex. To the Kingswood School
for Girls (plate 5), Loja contributed a remarkable ensemble
of rugs, draperies, and furniture coverings, executed by a
dozen weavers; Pipsan decorated the auditorium and the
dining hall interiors; and Eero, aged twenty, was responsible
for the vigorous furniture. For Eero this was an *oeuvre de
jeunesse* without lasting importance in his career, but his bold
handling of the wooden chairs reveals a sculptural bent which
long afterward would richly suffuse both his furniture and
architecture. At that time he seriously intended to become a
sculptor (as Eliel had wished to be a painter); and he spent
a year at the Grande Chaumière in Paris, only to return to
the United States to undertake formal architectural studies
at Yale. Of his sculpture almost none remains. One of the few
known pieces is a bust of his father (plate 6).

Like every major American school of architecture before
Gropius assumed control at Harvard and Mies at Illinois
Institute of Technology, Yale then was still a stronghold of
Beaux-Arts classicism. Eero nevertheless reacted to the eclectic program with characteristic resourcefulness and brilliance,
and the splendor of his drawings shows how his energetic
genius enlivened even an academic idiom. He graduated in

16 1934 with a wealth of honors and a traveling fellowship which took him back to Europe for two years. This time he assiduously contemplated cityscapes and buildings from Italy to Scandinavia: Piazza San Marco, Tuscan hill towns, Versailles (where he was fascinated by the fountains), the Gothic cathedrals ("to me Gothic is the greatest example of all things combined into one great thing: great engineering, but at the same time great form, great knowledge, great scale, great everything"), Haussmann's Paris ("a very beautiful city of street façades"), and, of course, the new architecture wherever it had arisen.

When he returned to Cranbrook, the long preparatory period was over, and he was ready to assume large responsibilities both in the school and in his father's architectural firm. He was twenty-six, soon to be married to Lily Swann (who was studying ceramics at Cranbrook), and he took his natural place as instructor of design and partner to Eliel.

Cranbrook, too, was entering a new phase. An extremely talented group of young designers had clustered about Eliel, among them Charles Eames, who had brought with him a generous belief in the possibility of a technological humanism. He and Eero became inseparable friends and collaborators. Harry Bertoia was in charge of metal crafts. Men as gifted as Harry Weese and Ralph Rapson came to learn architecture and city planning. But the main new force was Eero's. As he worked with his father on a number of challenging commissions, a clarification of form and simplification of means perceptibly emerged in their joint work. The buildings, to be sure, remained unmistakably Eliel's in their deliberate monumentality, use of water, and choice of materials. The Kleinhans Music Hall at Buffalo (1938), for example, achieved its heavy symmetries by the juxtaposition of large, but rather dull masses, and was as much a restatement of earlier motives as were the taut, freestanding campanile and noble nave of the Tabernacle Church of Christ in Columbus, Indiana (1940), which remains perhaps the purest exemplification of Eliel's long-standing dependence on contrasting horizontal and vertical forms (plate 9).

In basic programming and functional organization the buildings of this period represent a substantial step forward, as their floor plans reveal best. In clearly articulated classrooms of the Crow Island School at Winnetka, Illinois (1939), done in association with Perkins, Wheeler & Will, a more rigorous analysis of related spatial and practical needs than in any of Eliel's previous work became obvious (plates 7, 8). This new rigor, on the evidence of Eames' description of the firm's approach to the national competition for the Smithsonian art gallery in 1939, was due mainly to Eero. First Eero "thought out the whole thing carefully," Eames has recalled, "and then told us the first thing to do would be to make 100 studies of each element that went into the building. We would then pick the best, and never let our standards fall below that. Then we would make 100 studies of the combinations of each element. . . . Then 100 studies of the combinations of combinations. When the whole thing was finished, Eero was almost in tears, because it was so simple. And then, of course, they won the competition."

In this respect the luminous exhibition hall and flanking auditorium were Eero's, but the mood of the design—its dry dignity and classic restraint, its somewhat ponderous massing, its placidly monumental pool—remained Eliel's (plate 10). The building was never erected, but years later Eero remarked that, if the Smithsonian were to go ahead, he would redesign it completely in accordance with his mature thought.

Independence

In 1940, when Eero Saarinen and Charles Eames together won two first prizes in the Museum of Modern Art furniture competition, and the young designers—each about thirty years old—for the first time received international recognition, they were in fact already committed to a structural aesthetic that owed more to the Bauhaus than to the gentle tradition of Eliel's Cranbrook. Their now celebrated molded plywood chair (plate 11) was an Internationalist work of art: its stripped-down form perfectly expressed physical structure, and it also carried the promise of assembly-line production. This was not craftsmanship but industrial design.

Equally interesting in terms of Eero's development in the forties, however, was his attempt to arrive at a functionalist, economical architecture liberated from pictorial considerations. The tied, bow-string arches of the wooden opera house at Tanglewood (plate 12), built in 1944 but designed earlier, was a step in this direction, but two unexecuted projects in metal were more searching. These were a suspension structure for a community center (1941), which shows the influ-

18 ence of R. Buckminster Fuller, and an ingenious "unfolding house" (1945) with a flexible roof that could unravel according to need for additional space (plates 13, 14). Such technical exercises were refreshing in wartime when the Saarinens were saddened by the tragedy of Finland, and Eero went to Washington in 1942 to serve with the OSS. During this period he managed also to help his father with quietly competent war housing projects at Willow Run and Center Line, Michigan.

At the end of the war, although Eliel remained dominant, Eero assumed greater responsibility than ever before in an office which had become one of the most widely known in the country, and which was now entrusted with a series of very large commissions. By far the largest was from General Motors for a $20,000,000 Technical Center outside Detroit, but after preliminary plans were prepared, the project was temporarily dropped. There was also extensive campus planning at Antioch, Drake, and Stephens, as well as a monumental scheme for a civic center along the Detroit waterfront and a war memorial for Milwaukee.

It soon became clear that Eliel would never execute most of this work. The father was aging. He had been born in 1873, four years after Wright, and a decade before Gropius, Le Corbusier, and Mies. He clung to an outdated monumentalism which the son could no longer accept, and when another national competition was held in 1948 for the Jefferson Westward Expansion Memorial, Eliel and Eero entered separately.

The Jefferson competition was Eero's first great opportunity, and he intended to create a monument not only to the Virginian and the nation, but also to the modern age. Although he usually considered the "spirit" of a project independently from its purely mechanical "function," the two were here inseparable: the spirit *was* the function. But the long site, facing the Mississippi, was of crucial importance. Only from an integrated solution of the requirements of site and spirit, he reasoned, could come the necessary symbolic program; and all this had to be "locked together" by an appropriate structural system.

Before he visited the site, he had considered some kind of "open vaulted structure"—possibly a "Pantheon in lacework"—for he thought a rounded shape, even in the very poor memorial overlooking the Tidal Basin in Washington, "not wrong for Jefferson." Yet when he saw the site, he immediately rejected a dome because "it would not rise up from the levee. I was trying to reach for an absolutely permanent form—a high form. Stainless steel would seem to be the most permanent of the materials we have . . . the thing one could trust most." From such logic—and not, as some critics have charged, from "exhibitionism"—sprang the gigantic arch of shining steel, 590 feet high, which Eero only later realized would also be a symbolic "gateway to the West" (plates 129–134).

At last he had created a work of art that was "all one thing," and it .was an American work of art, comparable to the Washington Monument. For the Modern movement, which has long been rightfully wary of "monuments," the arch proves that such a celebration need not be a meaningless pastiche, but an act of the mind and the heart. When it is completed, this great structure will stand as one of the chief works of the age, for its scale is that of the civilized future.

By one of the ludicrous gaffes which sometimes complicate major events, the jury's telegram announcing the first prize award was mistakenly addressed to Eliel. The family broke out the champagne, as it invariably did on such occasions, and Eero toasted his father. A few days later the error was corrected, and then—like Shakespeare's Prince Hal—the heir wore his father's crown before the old king's death.

General Motors

"The son's contribution is in giving form or visual order to the industrial civilization to which he belongs, designing imaginatively and soundly within the new esthetics which the machine age demands and allows."

from "Now Saarinen the Son" by Aline
B. Louchheim, later Mrs. Eero Saarinen

"And then," Eero Saarinen would tell the story quietly, and rather shyly, knocking the ashes from his pipe, "General Motors came back." The huge corporation had been away for three years. During the interval its executives had gauged the feasibility of the technical research center for which the Saarinen firm had done preliminary studies in 1945, and by 1948, as General Motors prospered on the tremendous swell of unprecedented post-war sales, the dormant project was reactivated on a munificent scale. The buildings cost around $60,000,000, and the total project, including land acquisition and equipment, more than $100,000,000. General Motors had come to the Saarinens, Eero later recalled, "for another Cranbrook." Instead, he convinced them that the Technical Center should be an expression of a high-precision, mass-production, metal industry. Once the corporation grasped this concept, its formidable technological resources were placed at the service of the Saarinen firm and the associated architect-engineers Smith, Hinchman & Grylls. The buildings which resulted from this fusion of serious design and technological power were to be accurately described by *Architectural Forum* as "exalted industrial products."

General Motors made another decision—very enlightened for the time—to confide responsibility for the design to Eero when it became apparent that Eliel would never execute the vast project. The Technical Center would not be dedicated until 1956, six years after Eliel's death. By then Eero, largely because of his work for General Motors, would be one of the most highly respected architects in the world. Thus the Technical Center marked a crucial transition—a coming of age —for the new architecture, but its design was nevertheless firmly based on the structural esthetic developed by one of the chief members of the older generation, Ludwig Mies van der Rohe.

Since 1939, Mies van der Rohe had been steadily creating

an uncompromisingly modern environment for the Illinois Institute of Technology (plate 15), and his masterly campus powerfully affected the final design of the Technical Center. Yet the impoverished institution could afford none of the material splendor with which General Motors endowed its Technical Center; and the compressed, urban site of the Illinois Institute of Technology, bordered by a dismal Chicago slum, presented problems which did not confront Saarinen on the tremendous *tabula rasa* of the industrial plain at Warren, Michigan.

Eero Saarinen, then, was the first modern architect fortunate enough to work on a titanic scale without serious budgetary restrictions, just as he was the first of the younger Modernists to enjoy the chance (Skidmore, Owings & Merrill would have the second in the Air Academy) to apply the principles of their pioneer predecessors to a problem of this magnitude.

How sensitively and unaffectedly Eero Saarinen understood those principles is made immediately apparent by the first exhilarating view of the ensemble: the great, rectangular lake—1780 feet long, 560 feet wide—with the "water wall" fountain and Alexander Calder's smaller fountains in action and the stainless steel water tower rising as a gigantic technological sculpture at the northern end; the elegantly calibrated buildings, distributed in five main groups on three sides of the water, extending in long, evenly rhythmical façades of glass and metal, and halting abruptly in glazed brick end walls which are placards of glowing color, red, orange, yellow, tangerine, and a deeper red, and light blue and dark blue, gray and black. The structures, except for a low, glistening dome on the south, compose an assemblage of overlapping bright and neutral planes, which cannot be taken in at a single glance, but compel the eye to travel over water and lawns, from end to end of the 3000-foot-long composition—indeed to the limits of the square-mile site, which has been planted with 13,000 trees that eventually will enclose it as a forest (plates 16, 17).

Everywhere the architecture shows the skill and discipline of a polished but bold designer. This is functionalist architecture that transcends functionalism, as fine architecture always has, although the precise articulation of structure is based on clear technical needs. A five-foot module runs through façade after façade, and within the membranes of

22 glass the interiors—for the most part column-free—are also completely modular. Ceilings, like walls and floors, and with them air conditioning, illumination, and other mechanical equipment, are integrated in a multi-dimensional, rigorously consistent structural system which creates large areas of Miesian "universal" space that may be easily adapted to new use under the continuing impetus of the scientific-technological revolution of our times (plates 18, 20).

As Saarinen freely conceded, the direct influence of Mies can be detected throughout. Certainly the Technical Center would not have this specific form if the masterful, rectilinear campus of I.I.T. had not been designed earlier. This said, however, it may be noted at once that the festive mood of the Technical Center, including exuberant details such as the Calder "water ballet" fountains, the rather melodramatic spiral staircase of the Research Administration Building, and the staircase of the Styling Building (plates 19, 21) is anything but Miesian. For even though the master revealed a taste for opulence in a few luxurious commissions such as the Barcelona Pavilion, he never used water, color, and site plan and structure in quite this manner.

The Technical Center is a meeting place, not to say battleground, of the two great, conflicting traditions of the new architecture: its dominant objectivist philosophy and its richly diversified, and therefore less easily categorized, romantic subjectivity. That the two were combined with such adroitness in the Technical Center is perhaps its main strength, but also the source of perceptible weaknesses.

Seen from this historical vantage, the Technical Center is much less Miesian than is commonly supposed, and in fact belongs to the most liberal range of the International Style (which other second-generation Modernists such as Oscar Niemeyer have also explored). Although Saarinen's design acknowledges Mies as an unrivaled exemplar of the structural esthetic of steel—a material which happens to be preeminent in the automobile industry—it remains that Mies is neither the inventor of the metal-and-glass curtain wall, nor the first designer of interrelated planar forms. All this goes back to the early Modern movement, not only to buildings, but to ancillary works of art such as *de Stijl* painting, sculpture, and furniture. In this sense a full-fledged Internationalist monument of the 1920's such as the Bauhaus, is a common ancestor of both I.I.T. and General Motors (compare plates 22, 24). Even in Gropius' earliest work—the Fagus shoe factory of 1911, for instance—elements of Saarinen's curtain walls, such as the neutral spandrels, are anticipated (compare plates 23, 26).

This long-standing rationale of puristic forms, however, is only one side of General Motors. The other, frankly lyrical, leads directly to Eliel Saarinen, and from him back to the complete range of historical architecture. The earliest proposal for the Technical Center, submitted by both Saarinens in 1945, shows Eliel's persuasive influence on the basic concept (plate 28). The immense lake—asymmetrical in its arbitrarily tapering outline, but fundamentally the lake that was finally created—already unifies the entire composition. A tall water tower, also to receive an improved final form, appears as the vertical element indispensable in Eliel's designs. On the lake's periphery, separated from the water by roads which became much less obtrusive, the main divisions of the complex—Research, Service, Process Development, Engineering, and Styling—were approximately in their ultimate locations. A dome, sitting like a blister on the Styling Building, anticipates the dome finally erected. But in this early version the buildings badly lacked clarity, order, and structural vigor. Under Eliel's direction the Technical Center would have been a more closely knit, but muddled, continuum of unresolved forms. Open pictorialism governed the design of a structure so important as the Research Building, which was given an expressionistic air-foil shape, reminiscent of a "streamlined" car (plate 29).

The next version of the design, developed almost entirely by Eero in 1949, showed decisive improvement. The lake was straightened, in harmony with the spirit of the crisp Internationalist idiom of the redesigned buildings; and one notable new feature, which was unfortunately dropped from the final program, gave focus and force to the entire composition (plate 27). This was a ten-story office slab which would have risen from the lake on slender *pilotis*, and which is gravely missed in the Center as it stands today. If this elegant tower—a vertical form which nevertheless would have imparted broad horizontal emphasis to the spreading ensemble—had only been built, one of the most disturbing shortcomings of the design would have been eliminated. The emptiness of the long, open side of the lake is reminiscent of a de Chirico anxiety painting: the individual finds himself in an unpeopled abstraction of industrial civilization, strangely cowed by distant forms. Moreover, the coherence of the design, which can be made so imposing by photography, diminishes as the over-all effect is experienced.

It becomes apparent that the 132-foot water tower (which had been omitted from the 1949 concept as superfluous in the presence of the office building) and the 50-foot high "water wall" fountain are called upon to do the work of visual unification, and they are simply not equal to the task. Neither is the dome of the Styling group—an interesting feat of steel-plate shell construction—which is covered with glistening aluminum panels that, in a regrettable optical effect, appear to melt with both bright sunlight and moonlight, so that the round form lacks strong definition (plate 30).

Because these three special features—the water tower, the water wall, and the dome—are unable to exert visual supremacy over the ensemble, the Center suffers from excessive diffusion. It has been written, by way of praise, that these buildings can be fully appreciated only from a speeding automobile, and that is lamentably true. Yet architecture, as Giedion has written, should meet the essential human needs of "bare and naked man," and not merely appear to him as a technological exploit. Saarinen evidently tried to meet this need, at least in part, by embellishing his structures with the bright walls of specially glazed brick, which symbolically celebrate handicraft tradition as an enduring spiritual force in industrial society.

Paradoxically, however, this intention—praiseworthy in itself—fails in its architectural application. What matters in buildings such as these—as Mies demonstrated with consummate authority at I.I.T.—is their basic technological premise. Therefore, although Mies used brick with the utmost subtlety in his campus buildings, as a logical infilling for the steel frames, the weaker material was never given visual value which might compromise the dynamic effect of the metal structure (compare plates 31, 32). In the finest façades at General Motors, such as the splendidly proportioned form of the Dynamometer Building (plate 33), Saarinen, too, showed the proper subservient role of brick to steel, of vivid color to black strength, of irregular handicrafted texture to the fault-less order of fine industrial products. But elsewhere, vir-tually as a demonstration of Picasso's dictum: "We do it first, and then others make it pretty," the Miesian esthetic is need-

lessly softened, and its potential force further reduced by the
repetitive beat of the small, modular bay. At I.I.T., the entire campus, both buildings and spaces, were organized on a 24-foot module which governs the whole with lordly calm. Saarinen might well have used an even larger unit at General Motors.

Nevertheless the Technical Center is one of the first major triumphs of the new architecture in this country. Where else, in the early 1950's, could one see industrial technology brought to bear so imaginatively on so many vexing problems of contemporary design? With the help of the General Motors technical staff, Saarinen and his associates developed a number of ingenious structural devices, most notably a neoprene gasket, similar to that used in auto windshields, which solved the problem of leakage, and was remarkably easy and economical to produce, install, and maintain. The porcelain spandrels, of sandwich construction, were also the first of their kind, only two and a half inches thick, but providing good insulation, and also free of the "ripple effect" that previously marred such surfaces.

Over the decade, in curtain wall after curtain wall, the Saarinen firm would develop and explore these elements and many others, including the quality of the glass itself, so that their transparent façades would stand technologically in a class by themselves. But already they were recognized for their crystalline excellence. So resourceful an architect as Arne Jacobsen of Denmark frankly adapted their *parti* in his Rødovre Town Hall (plate 25). General Motors had set a new standard for industrial architecture and if it remained in itself imperfect, and even incomplete, Eero Saarinen one day might have returned to General Motors to do the office structure it still requires. Possibly some day another fine artist will come, as Bernini came to St. Peter's, and by a single majestic stroke bring the vast unfinished enterprise into final resolution.

Toward a Total Environment: Universities and Embassies

"We should stop thinking of our individual buildings. We should take the advice my father gave me, 'Always look at the next larger thing.' When the problem is a building, we should look at the spaces and relationships that that building creates with others. . . . In the process [the architect] will gradually formulate strong convictions about outdoor space—the beauty of the space between the buildings —and if he does, he will carry his conviction on to his most important challenge—how to build cities."

EERO SAARINEN, 1960

For an architect deeply concerned with the fate of the modern environment, who since childhood had been trained in urban theory, planning, and civic design, Eero Saarinen was strangely shy of the large city. Most of his life was spent in semi-rural or spaciously suburban surroundings. In Michigan he lived in a remodeled, century-old farmhouse, close to Cranbrook, and his office was not in Detroit but in the suburb of Bloomfield Hills, first in a trim structure of his own design, later—as the firm rapidly expanded—in nearby Birmingham, in large, temporary premises with a false colonial front, smack on the highway. When he decided to move east shortly before his death, he selected as his new headquarters an isolated pseudo-German castle overlooking water, just outside of New Haven.

Apart from the embassies in London and Oslo, his only major urban structures will be the Manhattan tower for C.B.S. and the Vivian Beaumont Theater for Lincoln Center, both very late designs. Otherwise, his role in reshaping the modern city was limited to the 1947 project for the Detroit Civic Center, a promising scheme done with his father, but which owed much to Le Corbusier, and would have produced one of the most imposing public spaces in the nation if the municipality had not foolishly discarded it (plate 34).

Had he lived another decade, Eero Saarinen probably would have been deeply engaged in the redevelopment effort now gaining momentum in American cities, to which Mies, I. M. Pei, Skidmore, Owings & Merrill, and other distinguished architects have already made substantial contributions. Yet he was wary of most urban renewal: "We have these tremendous redevelopment projects, well financed, scientifically planned. They all look good on paper. Then you see them when they are up, and you wonder whether they are

really better than what they replaced. . . . These are terribly
torn things, and in many cases the architecture is very bad."

What Saarinen wished to renew, maintain, and improve was the organic expression of the *civitas* which he found weakened or destroyed virtually everywhere in modern civilization, with one significant exception—the university campus. Here was a permanent environment, often encapsulated within surrounding megalopolitan squalor, and threatened by it, but nevertheless basically healthy and capable of new growth. "Universities are the oases of our desert-like civilization," he wrote, ". . . they are the only beautiful, respectable pedestrian places left." These were places where one could make a stand against onrushing chaos, and resist it by responsible design.

The firm grappled with every kind of campus problem from master planning to the design of dormitory and academic groups, auditoriums, chapels, and other single buildings; in the last ten years the over-all scope and distinction of this university work was probably unequalled in the United States. Nevertheless, its quality varied sharply.

Its level was usually as high as that of the pleasant dormitory complex at Drake University in Des Moines (plates 35, 36), in which uneven terrain is taken at full advantage and the unprepossessing, brick-surfaced buildings of tilt-up concrete slab construction, somewhat reminiscent of Eliel's work in their vertical fenestration, are tied together by bridges spanning the central pool, and above all by the liberal balance of the total mood. Yet other university work from the same office, sometimes done at the same time, is impossible to accept as the work of a major architect—for example, the interiors of the University of Chicago dormitories. This may be partly attributed to skimpy academic budgets, but it also reflects the tumultuous phase through which the firm passed under the tremendous pressures of major commissions and competitions.

A wealth of new work poured into what, a few years earlier, had been a ten-man atelier. The staff rose to fifty, and eventually surpassed ninety. Joseph Lacy, in charge of project management, had been a partner since the firm had been organized as Eero Saarinen & Associates in 1950. John Dinkeloo, in charge of technical development, working drawings, specifications, and construction supervision, was made an associate in 1951 and a partner in 1956. Once again the firm was doing all of its working drawings, which of necessity had been farmed out in the case of General Motors, but which Saarinen naturally wished to control in his own office. He had to train new designers to replace some of his most gifted early assistants who had struck out for themselves. The new men, brilliant as some of them were, did not immediately understand—as some of their predecessors had—"what Eero meant by a nod or a grunt." Inevitably, Saarinen briefly lost full control.

Possibly, with uncanny prescience, he tried to do too much in too short a time, but those projects to which he gave his main attention of course remained inventive and frequently powerful. Sadly enough, however, the largest single commission to follow General Motors—and comparable to it in potential significance—was never carried out, to the real loss of American architecture. This was to have been a new north campus for the University of Michigan at Ann Arbor, roughly the size of the old campus south of the Huron River, and devoted to the fine arts, engineering, and research. The master plan of 1953 shows an integration of buildings and spaces more richly compact than General Motors, on a more challenging site; and the square central plaza, descending in five terraced planes to a deeply set fountain, would have made a stirring civic space (plates 37A, 37B).

Yet when Saarinen actually had the opportunity to create a major public space at M.I.T., in the plaza which contains the auditorium and chapel completed in 1955, the result was partial architectural success and failure of civic design (plates 38, 39). Perhaps, as Saarinen later conceded, the two curvilinear structures, hermetically turned inward upon themselves, were "too egotistical." Certainly, as he himself pointed out, they needed a neutral frame, carrying forward the monumental cadence of Welles Bosworth's earlier neo-classicism, in order for their rounded forms to achieve true continuity in a strong existing environment. How he could so wrongly anticipate the effect of these carefully executed buildings, considered either singly or in relation with one another, is a paradox that recurs often at this phase of his career. Here, in truth, are two buildings which fundamentally oppose, rather than complement, one another. Each is sometimes taken as a starting point for Saarinen's later structural expressionism, but in the case of the auditorium this is visibly false. Its very absence of superimposed, sculptural "expression"—its effect of heavy downward motion rather than soar-

ing grace—may be attributed to its absolute structural premise. The building was not completely satisfactory to Saarinen,
who recognized that it lacked precise definition of scale, and
he never returned to the *parti*.

The auditorium's shell—the first thin concrete covering of
this size in the United States—is a pure geometric form, an
eighth of a sphere, and thus structurally in the same universalist family as the puristic cubes of Mies. The only distinction to be drawn is that concrete as a plastic material may
properly assume forms which would be irrational in steel.
Consequently, except in the ill-advised concealment of the
massive underground abutments on which the three points of
the shell rest, the auditorium can be recognized as closer to
the "correct" structural theory of Nervi (who does achieve
dynamic upward motion in his logical buildings) than to the
wild, but paradoxically heavy and downward moving structural rhetoric of the Guggenheim Museum. The auditorium's
interior, furthermore, is not manipulated Wrightian space,
but uncommitted space in which any number of functions
might be housed. It could serve as a ballroom rather than a
cleverly organized (but slightly forced) concert hall (plates
40, 41).

The chapel, on the other hand, is another sort of concoction
entirely. As a cylinder, it, too, is a basically pure form, but
it is also a hierarchical building invested with qualities that
preclude any but its foreordained use as a mystical shrine.
That the brick drum is magnificently lighted within by reflec-
tions passed upward through the low arches of varying di-
ameter that rise from the moat to coincide with the undulating
interior shell, only serves to call the entire structural esthetic
into question. This is sculpture, as much a hollowed-out solid
as a shell, in which light and shadow, roughened texture, and
the delicate—overly delicate—foil of Harry Bertoia's shim-
mering screen, have all been subjectively combined as an
image—an idolum—of religious experience (plates 42–45).
But this is also pictorialism, and faintly theatrical. To glance
backward in this Orphic manner has its obvious dangers, but
Saarinen persisted in his development of the theme. On the
Indiana prairie the pitched roofs of Concordia College rose
as a Scandinavian village, an austerely Lutheran tableau, like
a set in a Bergman film, just as solidly organized and equally
unconvincing (plate 46).

At this point, however, Saarinen took a step that remains

puzzling to anyone who knows his virile architecture: he moved, quite distinctly, toward decorativeness. In his Vassar dormitory, which was most appropriately aligned with its curving site, there are traces of neo-medieval eclectic devices, both in the nervously peaked crowns of the vertical window strips and in the interior archways (plates 47, 48). Similarly, this decorative impulse flowered, if that is the word, on an even larger scale in the University of Chicago Law School (plate 49).

Although the Law School meets the requirements of a demanding functional program with manly directness, and shows Saarinen's hand at its surest in the deft arrangement of staircases and lecture halls in the classroom wing, the architect's major preoccupation was the creation of an exterior which would live happily with the Gothic campus as a whole. As he well recognized, the University is one of the most successful eclectic environments in the country. Buildings erected years apart, by different architects, stand harmoniously side by side because, as Saarinen put it, "they all had a discipline larger than themselves: the Gothic." But as a Modern architect, committed to technological veracity, he could not resort to literal eclecticism, and therefore he chose the path that Minoru Yamasaki was also taking and which Paul Rudolph would follow at Wellesley: the parody of a neo-Gothic idiom. This excursion led to disaster at the very heart of his design, for he depicted the central library—a multi-story structure of rather gross reinforced concrete construction—as a single airy volume enclosed by opaque black glass, lacily finished at top and bottom in a zigzag profile punctuated by the thin finials of the aluminum mullions. At night, however, when the building is illuminated, these superficial distractions vanish, and the entire mirage is exploded (plate 50). Yet the virtues of the Law School are many. In over-all scale, massing, and limestone facings, and once again the generous use of water, it takes its place with tact, as Saarinen intended, in a permanent environment.

This had, of course, also been his intention in the design for the London Embassy on Grosvenor Square, which in 1956 won him the third of his three first prizes in the only Federal Government competitions of his lifetime (plate 51). Because of its location in a world capital, on a famous (but scarcely distinguished) square, this building has attracted considerably more attention than if it had been simply another Fed-

eral office block in Washington. Nevertheless, its more
subdued, three-sided counterpart in Oslo (designed for a
triangular site), walled with precast, structural frames of
greenish-black Norwegian granite, aroused no controversy at
all (plate 52).

In both cases the State Department stipulated that the
buildings should "create good will by intelligent apprecia-
tion" of their sites. This was an engaging diplomatic gesture,
but in the case of London largely spurious, for although
Saarinen was instructed to recognize the site's "Georgian"
character, English commentators irately pointed out that the
square's only character was that of four-sided enclosure,
which Saarinen weakened by not building on the full width
of his side, thus opening holes at two corners, and which he
further marred—one critic claimed—with a structure that
exported "prestige in the form of 'glamour.'" In reply
Saarinen argued that the building anticipates the *future* appearance of the square, which is to be rebuilt on the other
side in pseudo-Georgian style, and this consideration determined the mass, cornice height, and over-all silhouette.
Furthermore, he was designing not for Grosvenor Square
alone but for London. After days of walking through the city,
he decided that London is "black and white," and that its
prime material is Portland stone which weathers to a magnificent black and white. Therefore, he adopted a broken-up
façade recalling the vigorously indented mannerist fronts of
neo-Baroque palazzos, which he predicted would age in an
interesting way (plates 53–54). Saarinen also pointed out
that this effect was achieved by structural rather than orna-
mental means: the walls are bearing members, composed of
integral elements, and their strength makes possible the
column-free interiors of the upper floors (plate 55).

All this might be true, except that it is hard to see how the
strident gold-anodized aluminum trim (which Saarinen eu-
phemistically called "straw-colored") will ever weather
handsomely. Bronze would have been incomparably better,
and would have spared the building its aggressive flash. One
may wonder, too, if the fretted modeling of the façade, its
frilly hardness, and jazzy assonance, will ever soften harmoniously. Furthermore, if the walls do act structurally,
their treatment is scarcely straightforward: this is a forcing
of structural devices for decorative ends.

And beneath these objections, surging upward from the

still flowing springs of Modernist idealism, is the disturbing accusation that Saarinen—and with him the United States—had made a tragic compact with the *status quo*. "We wanted it to be *revolutionary*," protested the English architect Peter Smithson, "and we are puzzled why you . . . should accept such frozen and pompous forms as the true expression of a generous egalitarian society."

Why, indeed? Was the embassy the creation of man mastered by—rather than mastering—the least attractive features of American society? Was Saarinen, as an American critic wrote, merely a "stylist"? In London, as in so many of his buildings, the answer must wait, until fog and soot and rain and sun have done their work to the stone. But Saarinen could not wait, and pushed forward boldly, asking new questions, and providing still more questionable, and ultimately revolutionary, answers.

Search for Form: Expression and Overexpression

"Every period has the impulse to create symbols in the form of monuments. . . . This demand for monumentality cannot, in the long run, be suppressed. It will find an outlet at all costs."
SIGFRIED GIEDION

The situation facing Eero Saarinen and other leading American architects in the later 1950's was without parallel in the history of the Modern movement. Even in its heyday the Chicago School did not enjoy commissions of the grandeur now offered, almost as a matter of course, to the nation's serious designers. Whole branches of the Establishment had endorsed the new architecture. It was a far cry from the twenties and thirties, when most advanced designs were executed only on paper, for the fifties marked the appearance of outstanding Modern buildings throughout the country.

This triumph, for which the older generation had fought so courageously, was as sweet as the commissioning of Mies to do the new Federal complex in the Chicago Loop, but it had its painful—and peculiarly American—ironies. Beyond creating an architectural "star" system very like the Hollywood prototype, which could briefly elevate a designer as limited as Edward D. Stone to dazzling prominence, the national hunger for novelty and indiscriminate adulation of "genius" caused an outbreak of capricious design which by 1960 would be accurately dubbed "the new chaoticism." Yet the crisis in design—a crisis that is far from over either here or abroad—cannot be resolved by *static* adherence to the principles of the pioneers who differed strongly among themselves. Unprecedented materials and techniques, moreover, in Nervi's words, "have liberated man's structural imagination completely." That this is true, Le Corbusier—acting from a totally different premise—proved at Ronchamp as irrevocably as Nervi at Turin. A number of younger architects, however, especially Americans, took this freedom as license. An ex-Miesian formerly so devout as Philip Johnson could inquire somewhat plaintively. "Can't we just wander aimlessly?" His recent façadism shows to what destination this kind of picaresque adventure leads.

Therefore, foreign critics as discerning as Reyner Banham, glancing apprehensively at America's growing collection of epicene new buildings, which have been given a seductive sheen by this country's unmatched technology, can speak of the "U.S. ballet school" of architecture. Sometimes, partly on the evidence of his worst buildings of the fifties, but also because he, too, from a radically different position, shared Stone's and Yamasaki's opinion that Internationalist austerity was a "purgative" no longer required, Saarinen has been grouped with them. This is guilt by association. Rather than a saccharine architecture of "delight," Saarinen was seeking nothing less than a new monumental order, overreaching the "personal" architecture of the past to achieve in each building "a clear statement—an expression" that could be emblematic of modern civilization rather than a memorial to its architect.

Obviously, all depended on what he meant by "expression." As early as the first World War, the young Eric Mendelsohn conjured up grandiose visions of "elastic" forms which he inflated with unquenchable egotism, like so many architectural balloons (plate 112). To Saarinen, this was merely histrionic formalism, in which *literary* content—*illustrated*, for example, in the lens-like forms of an optical factory—dominated, and inevitably distorted, those *structural* and *spatial* meanings which are the essence of architecture. A superficial formal comparison of Mendelsohn's sensuous vaults and pylons with Saarinen's thus can be very misleading. The real antecedent for Saarinen's expressionism is found at the furthest opposite extreme of the Modern movement, inscribed in one of its canonical texts. "Architecture," wrote Le Corbusier in 1923, "is the masterly, correct, and magnificent play of masses brought together in light." That this is simultaneously a definition of heroic sculpture makes no difference, for Le Corbusier took care to stipulate that architecture "goes beyond utilitarian needs." More precisely, he added: "Art enters in."

But if, as Saarinen declared, Le Corbusier is the "Leonardo da Vinci of our time," Frank Lloyd Wright was to him "the Michelangelo" who "saw the building whole, as one organism, and . . . saw that organism in relation to its surroundings." Wright's architecture—at its most lucid—was always "all one thing," as Saarinen wished his own to be. "You can ask about Corbu's building at Marseilles—*is* it all one thing? Would Wright have put those peculiar sculptural forms on the roof the way Corbu did, or would he have integrated them with the total mass? . . . Corbu separates things, but they are held together by this terrific inventive spirit." Here were the masterly precedents, taken to heart by the thoughtful young architect who, as the fifties progressed and his own art rapidly matured (and as his personal happiness was bolstered by a remarkably compatible second marriage to the art critic Aline Louchheim), was to stride forward independently toward a new vision of organic wholeness.

Like all poetic visions, it was timeless, drawing upon the past, anticipating the future, although it was firmly grounded in the present, and at all times dependent on the machine technology of our industrial civilization. The works of this late period—only half a dozen years, really—bear analogies not only with the unified temple at Oak Park and the mystical chapel at Ronchamp, but also with the huge block of architectural sculpture that is the apse of Saint Peter's of Rome, the lifting vaults of Chartres, and the perfect civic presence of the Parthenon.

Each of Saarinen's buildings, no matter how it differed from the others in site, program, and especially, "spirit," was meant to be "all one thing." If studied as isolated flights of the imagination (which is the way the architectural press has commonly regarded them), they may appear erratic. Every one of these later structures is a radical statement, conceived as the total expression of an overriding—a supreme—central idea which germinated from a responsible (as opposed to egoistic) evaluation of its various requirements. Because these were major undertakings—in size and site as well as purpose—their expression is monumental. Insofar as most contained features widely applicable in an industrial civilization, they are also to some degree prototypical. And each, taken as the sum of its objective and subjective content, is a symbol.

To the diversity that such a method must produce, and to the tantalizing brevity of the period in which Saarinen was able to apply it, should be added the further critical problems raised by the existence of two parallel series of final structures: one in steel, the other in concrete, but both quite rightly "in the nature of materials." Each series leads—unevenly enough—to a masterpiece.

Expression in Steel: Precision and Flexibility
After General Motors, Saarinen's next industrial commission was for an electronics plant and accompanying administra-

tive facilities for International Business Machines outside Rochester, Minnesota (plate 56). Saarinen arrived in midwinter, accompanied by Kevin Roche, an extraordinarily gifted young Irish architect who had become chief of his design staff. Roche relates that Saarinen requested a small plane so that they could inspect the site, but only the pilot's windshield had de-icers, and their windows quickly froze over. Nevertheless, Saarinen remained in the air, smoking his pipe and thinking. He had seen enough. Half of the year this rich northern terrain was white. At other times it would be lush green. And there was the limitless blue of the sky. Architecture, he later remarked, consisted largely of "placing something between earth and sky."

Site demanded one thing, functional program another. On this second count I.B.M.'s needs were clear. The corporation required "maximum flexibility for growth," and its experience showed that expansion was likely to occur in self-contained areas of 60,000 square feet in manufacturing and 40,000 square feet in administration. Neither Saarinen nor I.B.M. (which had awakened to the advantages of handsome design in both products and buildings) wished these additions to be "random, parasitical, or wart-like." There must be harmonious order. This need for order led to the third indispensable quality of a Saarinen design: spirit. Not merely order but high efficiency should be expressed through structural precision and advanced building techniques, he reasoned, for this smokeless factory for electronic data processing equipment to belong, visually as well as functionally, to the Second Industrial Revolution.

From the three considerations grew another sweeping ensemble of rectilinear forms, much more densely integrated (because of a more concentrated program) than General Motors, but, like it, adhering to a clear definition of functional needs, branching east and west in an asymmetrical, but regularly predictable pattern from the central cafeteria and recreational pavilion. No matter how many large manufacturing blocks would be added in one direction, or smaller administrative units in the other, the whole would remain orderly and calm (plate 57). Moreover, in winter or summer, the blues of the long curtain walls would register with vibrant intensity in the midst of a white or green landscape, beneath a sky of different blue. The arbitrary division of the spandrels into areas of dark and light blue (signifying no internal dispositions) is patently unjustified (plates 58, 59). As at General Motors, Saarinen again relied on decorative color to achieve vitality that would have been better attained by structural means. The vigorous, large-span steel structure was consigned to the interior. These walls are in the truest sense curtains, supported by their own aluminum mullions, and merely acting as membranes which seal the interior volumes. The aluminum extrusions, five inches in depth, give an "accordion effect" when seen from different angles, showing a continuous silvery façade when viewed obliquely, and then suddenly opening in a blue expanse.

The wall is remarkable in its technical refinement: for its time this was the thinnest enclosure of such insulating value (equal to a 16-inch brick wall) ever developed (plate 60). The spandrels of "sandwich" construction here have become "wafers" only 5/16 of an inch thick (compared with $2\frac{1}{2}$ inches at General Motors). They are simply fine layers of aluminum, porcelainized on the exterior, which have been laminated to an asbestos core. The neoprene gasket has become a more efficient weatherseal than at G.M., and in virtually every other respect these surfaces are among the most economical ever devised. Nevertheless, they remain surfaces: two-dimensional planes in what might have been a three-dimensional composition of great depth.

In 1956, after the Rochester plant was designed, I.B.M. offered Saarinen an even more challenging commission for a research center on a splendid park-like site in Westchester County, New York, near the little community of Yorktown. Saarinen's earliest schemes for this project were "campus" and "village" concepts which he rejected when shortly afterward a similar but still more magnificent commission came from Bell Telephone Laboratories to design one of the largest research centers in the world at Holmdel, New Jersey. This huge facility, which also was to stand in isolated grandeur worthy of a Renaissance chateau, would eventually house 4,000 science workers in over one million square feet of space, half of it to be constructed in the first stage of the project.

Saarinen logically attacked both designs simultaneously, for the functional problems were similar if not identical. Each called for many small laboratories, studies, and other spaces in which exacting research was to be conducted under controlled conditions, and artificial lighting and air conditioning were mandatory. Furthermore, an incredible amount of elaborate, and frequently delicate, equipment—all subject to continuous rearrangement and revision—had to be installed. (Some spaces at G.M. had been 500 per cent reorganized within a decade.) Privacy for the scientists was essential, but so was convenient intercommunication; and Bell's experience at its badly extended Murray Hill facilities showed that neither is easily achieved in a vast research operation.

Symbolically, I.B.M., Yorktown, and Bell were also similar. Both were to be emblems of the forever unfolding science and technology which were inseparable from creative humanism. How deeply Saarinen's humanist art entered into these creations is revealed by the first lordly appearance of I.B.M.—"eyeing the valley," in Auden's line, "like a motionless eagle" from the crown of its circular hill (plates 61, 63). I.B.M.'s 1090-foot-long crescent of metal and glass—quite black and ribbon-like in the distance—is one of the majestic façades of modern times. As it is approached on the winding road, which Saarinen thoughtfully led through the hollow in which he created a little lake, the building vanishes momentarily—as do European hilltop monuments such as Vézelay —only to reappear with a sudden statement of scale, unexpectedly large and even formidable, as detail after eloquent detail comes into sight across the lifting terrain, to contribute to the sweeping grandeur of the façade.

This superb all-glass wall is the building's main source of power. Here the transparent sheath allows structure and volume to register tellingly, and therefore it succeeds precisely where the earlier curtain walls of Rochester and G.M. fail (plate 62). At Yorktown, where the walls enclose corridors rather than offices or labs, Saarinen was able to dispense with the horizontal spandrel by running the near-black glass from floor to ceiling. Only fine metal strips separate the triple bank of tall panes at the floor levels, so that the effect is of a continuous glass surface from the base of the building to the roof. The floors are vigorously defined by their recessed slabs, set back—in a particularly distinguished detail—fifteen inches from the glass. The ends of the façade, in contrast to the indecisive corners of G.M. and Rochester, are handled with unhesitating mastery in a return, crisply bent around the side of the building, to the end-walls of native fieldstone (plate 65).

The use of buff-colored masonry, which acts as a massive

foil for the patrician glass and the slender mullions (made to seem more slender by their relieving pencil-line of silver), is an exceptional tribute to the site. Although the walls are laid up with mortar, they resemble old Westchester County dry-walls, and in fact are largely taken from the Frostian pasture barriers which existed on the site. With robust romanticism Saarinen has used this stonework both within and without the building, contrasting it with sumptuous industrial materials. In places, however, this has been with insufficient conviction, as in the loose forms which curve counter to the building on either side of the entrance canopy (and which incidentally serve as perches for Seymour Lipton's badly overwhelmed sculpture that belongs indoors in some museum, see plate 64).

In general, however, the stonework serves to lodge the building solidly in the contour of the rising hill; and on the two-story rear façade, broad areas of masonry, exposed to the southern sun, help reduce the air-conditioning load. The back of the building is perceptibly less strong than the front, partly because the roof monitors come into view too prominently, but mainly because of the sugary Japanesque garden which Saarinen unaccountably allowed landscape architects Sasaki, Walker & Associates to create (plate 66).

Once inside the curving structure, it becomes apparent that its form—admirably given to further expansion around the top of the hill—is the result of a logical program as well as an expression of the site. Although this is a glass building, it is also a building without traditional windows. Behind the tremendous façades run circulation galleries that may be compared with the glazed promenade decks of ships. The laboratories and offices do not front on them (except for special spaces such as the handsome library), but instead are interior rooms—really, partitioned spaces in modular cross-blocks—which face on transversal corridors, and back on structural service spines in which the complex utilities system is housed (plate 67).

In theory this plan may seem forbidding, but in practice it is thoroughly sound, and does credit to Saarinen's policy of painstaking research. Before adopting this concept he studied many laboratories, such as Bell's Murray Hill, and found that the window blinds were usually drawn. The corridors were double-loaded with traffic and equipment, and were commonly noisy and unattractive. Here the corridors are quiet and short, so that the great outer galleries are never more than seventy-five feet away. These luminous outer passages, with their breathtaking views of the countryside, are a triumph of spatial design, never oppressively long, because only a portion of their curving extent is visible at one time (plates 68, 69).

Bell Laboratories, nearing completion on a broad New Jersey plain, promises to be even finer than I.B.M., Yorktown, and perhaps will be one of the influential buildings of the age, for its *parti* is adaptable to any level emplacement. Later architects will find it difficult, however, to surpass the splendor of Bell's palatial baroque park which, in this country at least, is unrivaled as a formal setting for a technological building (plate 70). At the heart of the immense central ellipse, as the focal point of the tree-framed, water-enriched, expanding perspectives, the powerful monument—a 135- by 700-foot superblock which eventually will be joined by a second block in a single display of mass—was conceived by Saarinen as a gigantic mirrored cube, enclosed by expanses of silver-reflecting glass playing lavishly with light (plate 71).

Unlike I.B.M., Yorktown, this structure will have no associations with the pre-industrial past, except in its classic proportions and the grand, symmetrical harmonies of the park. Its immense interior will be magnificently flexible. The unprecedented "mirror glass," invented expressly for this project, was sought by Saarinen mainly to reduce the air-conditioning load (for it will reflect away approximately 75 per cent of the sun's heat). Yet, like most technological advances, this one carries with it the possibility of an advance in esthetic expression which Saarinen unerringly seized. These softly gleaming laboratories, everywhere organized with quiet perfection, will be a civilized beacon of human knowledge.

Because Saarinen could adopt a cubical concept of extreme simplicity at Bell, its functional program was expressed in more purely architectural terms than at Yorktown. The logical rectilinear order of the internal laboratory blocks makes them rigorously consistent with the discipline of machine-made materials and modular utilities. Although these interiors are essentially the same as I.B.M.'s, also girded by

analogous outer galleries, they have gained appreciable
clarity and directness (plates 72, 73).

Bell is a work of fully matured genius, and suggests how far Saarinen might have gone in this objective idiom. In contemplating Bell's plain-spoken design, however, one must also ponder the subjective inner convictions which caused the architect, in his last important design in metal and glass, to resort to overstatement—exaggeration—in the headquarters for Deere & Company that will be completed next year in a wooded valley near Moline, Illinois (plate 74). "An iron building for a farm machinery manufacturer," was Saarinen's summary of the concept. The phrase is straightforward enough, but it implies a welling romanticism that may be as poignant as an old harrow rusting in the American landscape. This building, too, will rust, but only to a shallow depth, for its high-tensile steel alloy—previously employed in engineering projects, but never before in fine architecture—oxidizes to acquire a darkly reddish, protective patina. It is also very strong, carrying the approaches to the main office building across the ravine on 120-foot trusses that need no diagonal bracing, and furthermore permitting extreme fineness of columns, beams, and other structural members, so that the interior will be remarkably open and light (plates 75, 76).

Nevertheless, Saarinen embellished this spare structure with extra steel in the form of rhetorical outriggers, so that the building's steel-like quality would be more fervently expressed. These have been described as sunbaffles, but they are employed on all sides of the building, which—it should be noted—will receive additional solar protection from mirror glass, similar to Bell's, but gold-tinted rather than silver (plate 75). Poetic intentions are obviously dominant here, and they find an analogy—as Saarinen was well aware—in Mies' use of heavy I-beam mullions in works such as the Lake Shore apartments (where lighter members would have been adequate). But Saarinen's expressionism is considerably less lucid, at least as it appears in model form, and the completed building will have to justify the concept. Whether it will seem as significant as Bell is a question which brings the whole purpose of the new architecture under review. Yet this is the very question asked by Saarinen in all of the remarkable concrete buildings designed late in his career, without which Deere's romantic structure of steel cannot be fully understood.

Concrete—a material which, if properly reinforced or pre-stressed, combines the compressive resistance of artificial stone, the tensile strength of steel, and the plasticity of poured cement—was irresistible to an architect who once wished to be a sculptor. Even in steel at General Motors, the cylindrical exhausts of the Dynamometer Building (plate 33) are treated as freestanding icons of industrial civilization, and other departures from rectangular discipline—the subtle curve of a roadway, the upsweep of an entrance canopy—show Saarinen subjectively carving the environment in the midst of a highly controlled technological order.

In his furniture, too, this drive toward plastic expression had never been still. The shapely "womb chair"—mark the frankly feminine name—of 1948 (plate 77) was followed by the voluptuous—and quite Corbusian—General Motors deep easy chair (plate 78), and then by the suavely sculptural "pedestal" furniture of the fifties, in which the cast aluminum base—the indispensable stabilizing element—is indistinguishable from the light plastic upper portions of a chair or table (plate 79). To Saarinen it mattered only that this furniture felt right and looked right, that—either as an individual piece or as part of an ensemble—it should be "one thing."

But sculptural structure is a very different affair when conducted on a monumental scale, and in his buildings Saarinen approached the same thesis cautiously. Although the first Jefferson Memorial design of 1948 (plate 129) was of partly subjective inspiration, it was also a stroke of rational structural functionalism: a catenary arch which, geometrically, was as predictable as a circle. The steel-plate shell of the G.M. dome (plate 30) and the concrete shell of the M.I.T. auditorium (plate 38) are governed by the same geometric purism, and thus absolutely subject to the laws of what Nervi calls "Building Science."

Both of these spherical forms leave much to be desired. G.M. fails to rise as a dome should, although its logic is faultless; and M.I.T. has been best criticized by Saarinen himself. "Theoretically," he remarked in 1960, it is "a very graceful building. Structurally, it's quite a rational building. But, if you look at it, isn't it a little bit too earthbound? The movement, the inevitable movement of an arch form, seemed to be downward: it did not have the soaring quality or sense of lightness that one wanted." Geometry, as Saarinen came to believe, needed energizing if it was to serve the spatial-struc- tural-spiritual totality he wished to *express*. This really meant *overexpression*.

Saarinen never wrote out his own expressionist theory although he did revise Sullivan's dictum "form follows function" to say: "function influences but doesn't dictate form." Like his friend Matthew Nowicki, another brilliant member of the new generation who died tragically, Saarinen shared Matisse's opinion that "exactitude is not truth." Nowicki— the designer of the seemingly objectivist, cable-slung inclined arches of the cattle-judging pavilion at Raleigh, North Carolina (plate 80)—was a spokesman for a number of young Modernists, Saarinen included, when he wrote before his death in 1960: "Art tends not only to discover the truth but to exaggerate and finally distort it. And, maybe in this distortion lies the essence of art."

Such adherence to the primacy of personal imagination, at a time when it was already perceptible that enormous social and technological forces are impelling architecture toward universalist canons, was a brave statement of the humanist position. Saarinen, too, of course, refused to accept a deterministic architecture; and possibly in this respect, as Peter Carter implied in a penetrating essay, his thinking was indeed "pre-technological." But perhaps it will outlast our still largely paleotechnic era, and find itself fully at home in a future biotechnic age.

Nevertheless, to distort subjectively the dominant objective realities of our time is to run grave risks of misinterpreting those realities. The design of Deere (plates 74–76) thwarts the inexorable logic of steel, a material which cries out for taxing structural tasks. In concrete, however, Saarinen had a yielding material that enabled him to broaden the emotional content of his buildings with supple power. Gradually, as the fifties progressed, this subjective motive bubbled upward, as in the nine low domes of the Irwin Union Bank & Trust Company in Columbus, Indiana (plates 81, 82). There was genuine architectonic energy at work here, giving a quiet monumental lift to an important building in a small town.

This energy next erupted in the massive form of a major monument for a large city: the Milwaukee War Memorial, completed in 1957 (plate 83). The symbolically militant, cross-shaped superstructure, jutting outward above the neutral, stone-sheathed pedestal in four great wings generated from a central court, can be seen as a single, spectacular abstraction of valor. Obviously, however, it is also a utilitarian building that performs complex service for the community as a "living" memorial. The separation of the upper and lower structure is justified by a division of purpose: the solid base contains an art gallery (which lacks natural light); the top contains the meeting rooms and offices of the veterans' center. This arrangement further provided the intermediate terrace —an heroic commemorative stage—where the names of the war dead are inscribed on the granite coping of the pool, and off to the east—beyond the dynamic, tapering pylons, which present different side and front elevations—extends the timeless expanse of the lake (plate 84).

Thus functioning program and the sloping, lakefront site have been integrated with the spiritual concept; and although the structural expression and cruciform plan have literary overtones, they, too, upon examination, reveal logical consistency within the needs of the design. The compressive strength of concrete is brought strongly into play by the egg-crate form of the upper structure. The very considerable cantilever—$29\frac{1}{2}$ feet—was facilitated by an ingenious system of reinforcement devised by the engineers Ammann & Whitney, in which steel rods at the top of the building take major tensile forces, counterbalancing the wings. To be sure, spaces of the same size could have been enclosed more directly and lightly in steel, or a three-dimensional grid of prestressed concrete, but the subjective expression of almost pugnaciously poised mass—the visible triumph over obstacles —might have been lost (plates 85–87).

Milwaukee—like its rather poor cousin, the University of Chicago dining hall (plate 88)—apparently suffered from Saarinen's personal loss of interest when he was intensely involved in the London Embassy competition. Many of the War Memorial's features, such as the stairway which mars the court, he later acknowledged could have been improved. Yet the building's "rightness" pleased him, and he plunged forward into two more notable projects that further investigated the sculptural potentialities of concrete.

The T.W.A. terminal at Idlewild was commissioned in 1956, shortly before the Ingalls hockey rink at Yale, but the rink at every stage advanced more quickly, not to say hastily, and was finished in 1958. The terminal's design and construction continued very slowly until 1962, and therefore it was af-

fected by Saarinen's experience with the rink. Although the
buildings differ in purpose, site, structure, and date, they belong together in mood. The rink expresses the exhilaration of
"an exciting game"; the terminal, "the drama of flight and
the excitement of travel." Both are "nonstatic" creations,
and in this respect avowedly are related to the Baroque, although they are free from classical discipline. Their structural forces have been intentionally set in motion, and then
accelerated, in order to enrich spatial and emotional content.

In both structures, Saarinen strove to attain the soaring
grace that eluded him at M.I.T. As at Milwaukee, he depended upon engineers—Fred Severud for the rink; Ammann & Whitney for the terminal—to ensure the structural
feasibility of these subjective *tours de force.*

The rink in particular is a prodigious effort. Swelling upward on the spine of its tremendous parabolic arch, and
swooping downward to either side in a concave, suspended
roof which is anchored to curving side-walls that repeat the
profile of the arch, with every other feature of the design—
the cantilevered reverse curves of the arch; the canted, sinu-
ous spurs of the end-walls flowing away from the tented
entrances—either flexed or loosened in a multi-directional
surge of plastic energy, the arena is never at rest, but charges
about its independent site with huge *brio.* As engineer Severud has written, it expressed "the tug-of-war between pull
and resistance"—a game more tumultuous than hockey
(plates 89, 90).

The game is innocent enough, but the rules have not been
absolutely enforced. On either side, three bracing cables run
from the arch to the base of the monument to guarantee sta-
bility under uneven loads of wind or snow. These independent
wires, like Renaissance tie-rods, weaken the entire structural
impact because of their thin linear value. Other exterior
shortcomings are the bulbous ventilating monitors which receive unwarranted prominence and the sullen black of the
neoprene weatherproofing. But as one is drawn—pulled—
through the compressed, hovering entrance, the interior enlarges suddenly in a high, bending volume, which the muscular arch negotiates in a 228-foot bound, with the wooden roof
lightly flying above the white sheet of ice. The use of wood is
questionable—it appears too easily flung upward—but the
space lives, as Saarinen intended, and perhaps justifies the
superenergizing of structure, even in so small an arena,

46 which seats only 3000 in the intimate stands, and could have been vaulted by much simpler methods. For without question this space is literally one of the most stirring in American architecture (achieved, it is true, like the space beneath the chained dome of Saint Peter's, with some loss of structural purity); but it would have been more stirring had certain details been more carefully designed (plate 91).

A low utilities block, for instance, has been allowed to mask one foot of the arch; the heating equipment is unsightly; the plaster soffit required by fire code spoils the encounter of the wooden ceiling and the heavy concrete base; the hung lamps act as a disruptive plane of brightness in a non-planar space. Yet none of these flaws overcomes the uninhibited vitality of the whole, and Saarinen was delighted by a goalie's appraisal: "Go, go, go!"

The architect, still gaining momentum, hurried forward with new gusto, unaware when the rink was finished in 1958 that he had only three years remaining, and eager to extend his spatial-sculptural thesis in T.W.A. There was now a rather large number of significant nonrectilinear structures, both here and abroad, which he could study in his quest for a valid plastic idiom. He of course could draw on the objective tradition of the engineers—Maillart, Freyssinet, Nervi, Torroja—but even Torroja, in his Caracas resort project, had sculpted a subjective group of irregular shells, thus approaching the terrain of the later Wright and Le Corbusier, who in turn had been long aware of visionary schemes of the sculptors, such as Naum Gabo's 1931 design for the Palace of the Soviets, in which ceilings and floors were conceived as opposed, elongated shells, very like the partly opened shell of a bivalve (plate 92).

In America alone, apart from the newly completed Guggenheim Museum, there were shells such as the interlocking barrel vaults of Minoru Yamasaki's St. Louis airport which, admirable as it is, from Saarinen's point of view left something to be desired as a flight terminal. Its domical form acted to fix the individual beneath it so that one did not wish to move on. St. Louis also showed that every detail of a curvilinear building must be subjected to a complete discipline, else discordance will result (plate 93). Even in the Guggenheim, Saarinen noted, Wright's extraordinary three-dimensional vision (and almost compulsive consistency) failed him in some unresolved corners.

To make certain that T.W.A. would be totally resolved—
"one thing"—Saarinen relied on model design to a degree
probably unparalleled in the contemporary movement, and
he found the method so rewarding that it was elaborated
steadily in later projects. The façade of London had been
drawn on paper, like a Renaissance façade, but sculptural
structures such as T.W.A. involved "completely new vocabu-
laries" which were molded, patterned, sculpted, in cardboard,
wire, and other materials before they could be even rendered
in two dimensions (plates 94, 96). Gradually, according to
the dictates of the site—a curving corner of the Idlewild
complex, directly in the path of one of its main axial lines—
and Saarinen's subjective interpretation of the program, the
design gathered drama as an essay in motion (plate 95). The
structure, lifting so rapidly from its widely splayed supports
that it appeared to be taking leave of the ground, was mis-
taken by some as a Mendelsohnian depiction of a giant bird.
In fact, it was meant only as an abstraction of spatial liberty,
expressed in continuous movement beneath the soaring roof
(plates 97, 100, 102).

The building was thus conceived as an emotional instru-
ment, resounding with monumental harmonies. The traveler
would feel the unfolding power of its symphonic motive as
soon as he passed through the aspiring front supports—massive sculptures in themselves—and then he would be carried
forward through the melodic entity, without a break in mood,
upward on convergent stairs into the crescendo of the central
space. Beneath the flaring shells—two pairs of segmented
barrel vaults, on cross axes, and separated from one another
by strips of glass—the terminal was designed as a totality of
fluid form, curving and circling within itself, in balconies and
softly drawn apertures, stairs and counters. Through the
enormous convex windows, slanting upward and outward,
there would be elating views of the runways and the sky; and
in the original design, glazed bridgeways—springing from
the main building to the heraldic departure stations—would
have been equipped with moving sidewalks to complete the
kinetic effect (plates 98, 99, 101).

The design was one of the most electrifying to be published
in the late fifties, but as construction slowly progressed in
1961 and 1962, it became clear that Saarinen's tonal vision
would come only partly true. The shells were conservatively
engineered by Ammann & Whitney (one wonders if a radical

48 system of prestressing along the principal lines of tension was ever considered); and the structure, far from ascending weightlessly, was heavily thrust in the air—heavily, at least, in comparison with Felix Candela's airy coverings of large areas. Although photography enlarges the scale of T.W.A., it is in fact a rather small building, only 322 feet long and 222 feet wide at its furthest extremities. Its eloquence seems too rich for the content of the problem and in the context of its surroundings. If T.W.A. stood alone on a green hill as a non-utilitarian shrine, it might have been a more successful building. Unfortunately, it happens to grace one of the more vulgar architectural circuses yet staged by the Modern movement, and in the midst of the commercialized structural exhibitionism of Idlewild, in which every building clamors for attention at the expense of the whole, Saarinen's undoubted sincerity suffers.

T.W.A.'s failure, then, was part of much broader failings of our irrationally driven society. Idlewild—as Saarinen came to know better than anyone else long before T.W.A.'s completion—was predicated on wrong notions of architectural and operational rivalry. Individual man, in the symbolic personage of the traveler, was given less consideration, on the whole, than were machines and corporations. None of these terminals (T.W.A. included, now that its bridgeways have been executed as oppressively enclosed tunnels and the moving sidewalks discarded) conveys the passenger to his plane as he should be: a citizen of a logical world order based on the ever-changing nature of industrial civilization. Functionally and symbolically, Idlewild is already out-of-date, made obsolete, in truth, by Saarinen's own consummate masterpiece: the jet-age international airport for Washington.

1. *Eliel Saarinen. "Hvitträsk," Finland, 1902. Studio-living room.*

3. *Sketch of Eero by Eliel.*

2. *Eliel and Eero, 1919.*

4. *Eliel Saarinen. Cranbrook School for Boys,*
    Bloomfield Hills, Michigan, 1925–26.

5. *Eliel Saarinen. Kingswood School for Girls, Bloomfield*
    Hills, Michigan, 1929. Dining hall.

6. *Bust of Eliel by Eero.*

7. *Saarinen and Saarinen, Perkins, Wheeler & Will. Crow Island School, Winnetka, Illinois, 1939. Main-floor plan.*

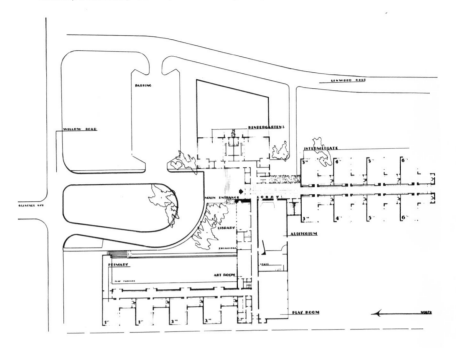

8. *Crow Island School. Exterior.*

9. *Saarinen and Saarinen. Tabernacle Church of Christ, Columbus, Indiana, 1940.*

10. *Saarinen and Saarinen. Smithsonian Institution, 1939, project. Model.*

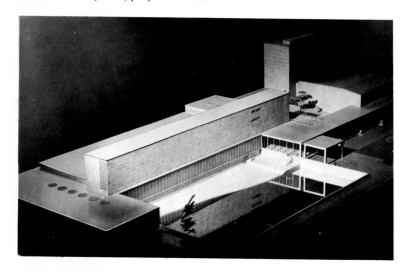

11. *Eero Saarinen and Charles Eames. Organic design chair, molded plywood with sponge rubber, 1940. (Collection Museum of Modern Art.)*

12. *Saarinen and Saarinen. Tanglewood Opera House, Lenox, Massachusetts, 1944.*

13. *"Unfolding house," 1945, project. Model.*

14. *Community Center, 1941, project. Model.*

15. *Mies van der Rohe. Illinois Institute of Technology, 1940. Model.*

16. *General Motors Technical Center. Site plan.*

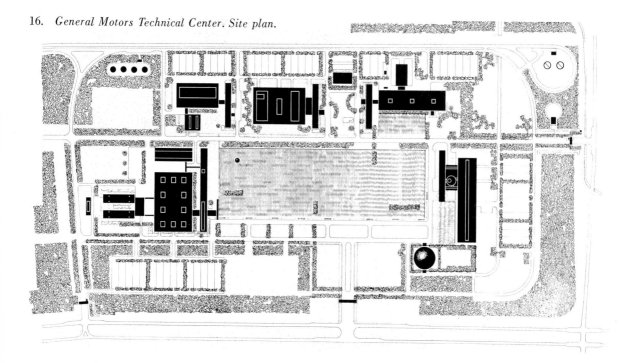

17. *General Motors Technical Center, Warren, Michigan, 1951–57. View showing lake and water tower, with Styling Auditorium and Administration Building in background. (Photo: Ezra Stoller)*

18. *General Motors Technical Center.*
    Industrial space. (Photo: Ezra Stoller)

19. *General Motors Technical Center. Staircase*
    in Styling Administration Building.

20. *General Motors Technical Center. Drafting room. (Photo: Ezra Stoller)*

21. *General Motors Technical Center. Spiral staircase in Research Administration Building.*

22. *Walter Gropius. Bauhaus School, Dessau, 1925–26. (Photo: Museum of Modern Art, New York)*

23. *Gropius and Meyer. Fagus Factory, Alfeld, Germany, 1910–14. (Photo: Museum of Modern Art, New York)*

24. *General Motors Technical Center. Glazed bridgeway. (Photo: Ezra Stoller)*

25. *Arne Jacobsen. Town Hall, Rødovre, Denmark, 1955.*

26. *General Motors Technical Center. Process
Development Administration Building.*

27. *General Motors Technical Center, 1949.
Aerial perspective by J. Henderson Barr.*

28. *Saarinen and Saarinen, General Motors Technical
Center, 1945. Aerial perspective by Hugh Feriss.*

29. *Saarinen and Saarinen, General Motors Technical Center, 1945.
Rendering by Hugh Feriss.*

30. *General Motors Technical Center. Styling Administration Building at left,*
Styling Auditorium in background. (Photo: Ezra Stoller)

31. *General Motors Technical Center. Service Administration Building.*

32. *Mies van der Rohe. Illinois Institute of Technology,*
    Minerals and Research Building, 1942–43.

33. *General Motors Technical Center. Dynamometer Building. (Photo: Ezra Stoller)*

34. *Saarinen and Saarinen. Detroit Civic Center, 1947, project. Model.*

35. *Dormitory complex, Drake University,*
    Des Moines, Iowa, 1951–55.

36. *Drake University. Site plan.*

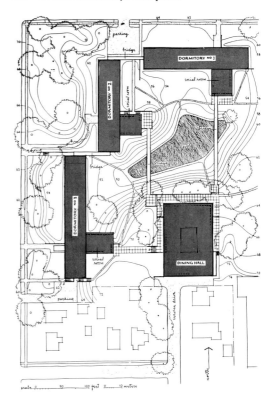

37A. *North Campus, University of Michigan, Ann Arbor, 1953, project. Site plan.*

37B. *University of Michigan. Rendering.*

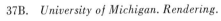

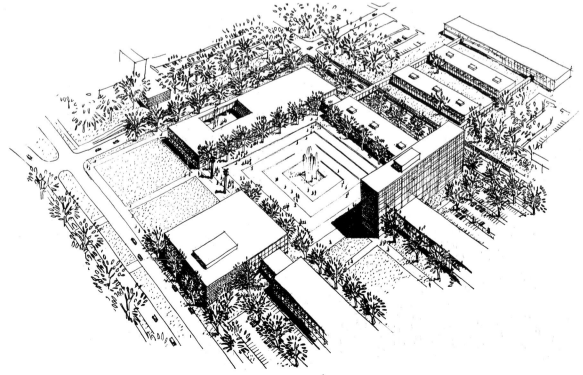

38. *Kresge Auditorium and Chapel, Massachusetts Institute of Technology, 1955.*

39. *M.I.T. Site plan.*

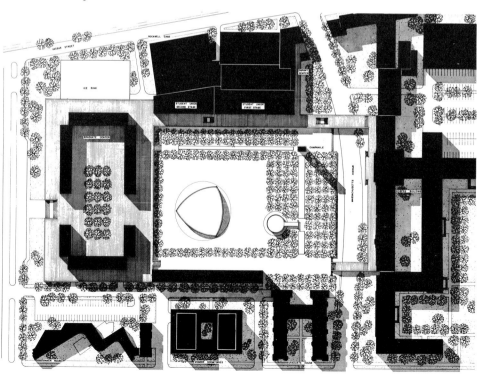

40. *M.I.T., Auditorium. Exterior.*

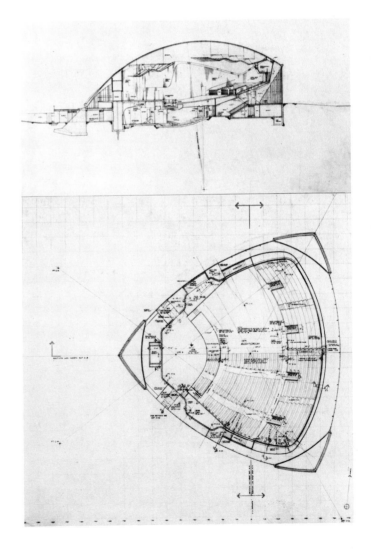

41. *M.I.T., Auditorium. Plan and section.*

43. *M.I.T., Chapel. Plan.*

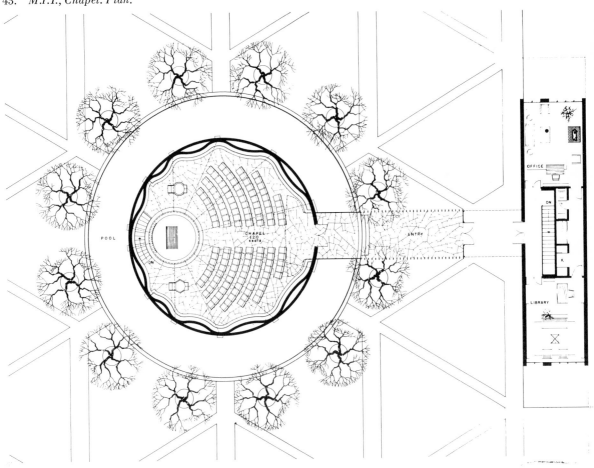

44.   *M.I.T., Chapel. Interior. (Photo: Ezra Stoller)*

45.   *M.I.T., Chapel. Interior detail. (Photo: Ezra Stoller)*

46. *Concordia College, Fort Wayne, Indiana, 1953–58.*

47. *Emma Hartman Noyes House, Vassar College, Poughkeepsie, New York, 1954–58. Exterior.*

48. *Emma Hartman Noyes House. Interior.*

49.   *University of Chicago Law School, Chicago, Illinois, 1956–60. Exterior.*

50.   *University of Chicago Law School. Night view.*

51. *U.S. Embassy, London, 1956. Main façade.*

52. *U.S. Embassy, Oslo, 1955–59. Main façade.*

53.   *U.S. Embassy, London. Detail of façade.*   54.   *U.S. Embassy, London. Detail of façade.*

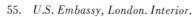
55.   *U.S. Embassy, London. Interior.*

56. *International Business Machines, Rochester, Minnesota, 1956. Aerial view.*

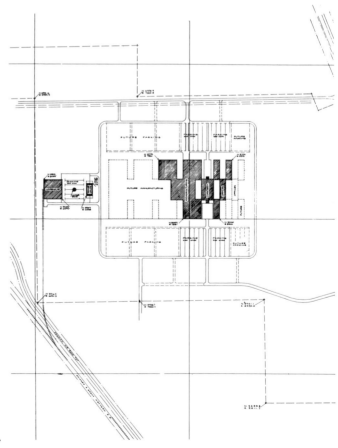

57. *I.B.M., Rochester. Site plan.*

58. *I.B.M., Rochester. Curtain wall detail.*

59. *I.B.M., Rochester. Curtain wall and corner.*

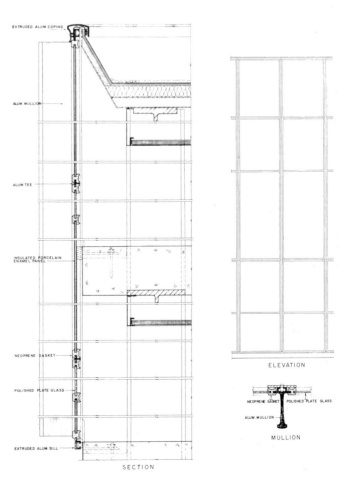

60. *I.B.M., Rochester.*
Mullion detail and section.

61.   *International Business Machines, Yorktown, New York, 1956. General view.*

62.   *I.B.M., Yorktown. Approach façade.*

63. *I.B.M., Yorktown. Site plan.*

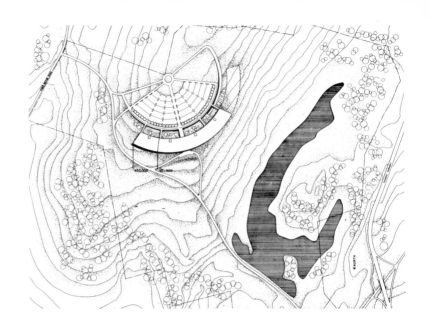

64. *I.B.M., Yorktown. Entrance with Lipton sculpture.*

65. *I.B.M., Yorktown. Corner detail.*

66. *I.B.M., Yorktown. Rear view. (Photo: Ezra Stoller)*

67. *I.B.M., Yorktown. Floor plans.*

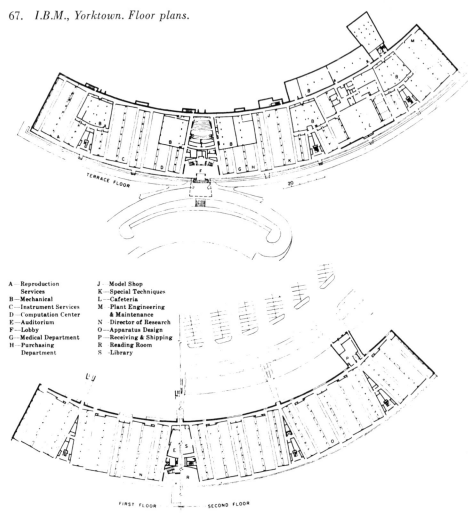

TERRACE FLOOR

A — Reproduction Services	J — Model Shop
B — Mechanical	K — Special Techniques
C — Instrument Services	L — Cafeteria
D — Computation Center	M — Plant Engineering & Maintenance
E — Auditorium	N — Director of Research
F — Lobby	O — Apparatus Design
G — Medical Department	P — Receiving & Shipping
H — Purchasing Department	R — Reading Room
	S — Library

FIRST FLOOR   SECOND FLOOR

68. *I.B.M., Yorktown. Interior corridor.*

69. *I.B.M., Yorktown. Outer gallery.*

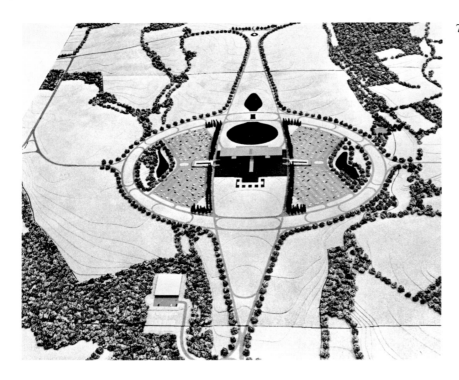

70. *Bell Laboratories,*
Holmdel, New Jersey.
Under construction.
Site model.

71. *Bell Laboratories. Model. Main façade.*

72. *Bell Laboratories. Interior.*

73. *Bell Laboratories. Floor plan.*

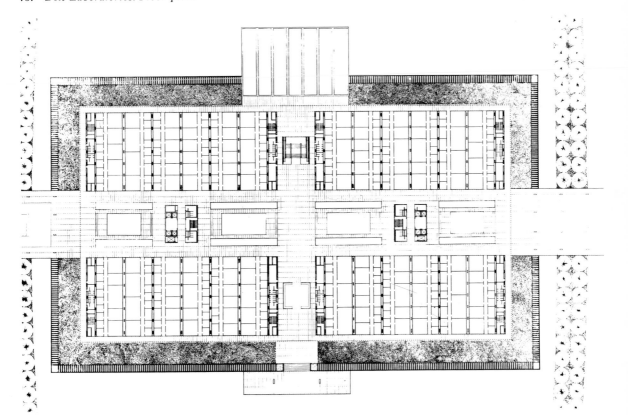

74. *Deere and Company, Moline, Illinois.*
      Under construction. Site plan.

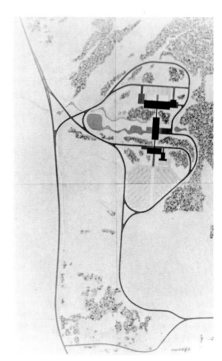

75. *Deere and Company. Mock-up.*

76. *Deere and Company. Model.*

77. *"Womb chair," molded plastic and
foam rubber, 1948. (Collection Museum of
Modern Art, Gift of Knoll Associates.)*

78. *General Motors Technical Center. Engineering
Lobby, showing "deep easy chair."*

79. *Pedestal furniture, 1955–57.*

80. *Matthew Nowicki in association with William Henley Deitrick. Cattle-judging pavilion, Raleigh, North Carolina, 1953.*

81. *Irwin Union Bank and Trust. Interior.*

82. *Irwin Union Bank and Trust, Columbus, Indiana, 1952–55.*

83. *Milwaukee War Memorial, Wisconsin, 1957. Exterior seen from the park.*

84. *Milwaukee War Memorial. Terrace, view toward lake.*

85. *Milwaukee War Memorial. View of lakeside façade.*

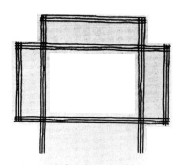

86. *Milwaukee War Memorial. Structural diagram.*

87. *Milwaukee War Memorial.*
   Detail under cantilever.

88. *Dining Hall, University of Chicago, Chicago, Illinois, 1955–58.*

89. *Ingalls Hockey Rink, Yale University, 1956–58.*

90. *Ingalls Hockey Rink. End view. (Photo: Ezra Stoller)*

91. *Ingalls Hockey Rink. Interior. (Photo: Ezra Stoller)*

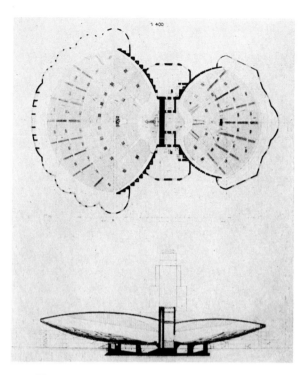

92. *Naum Gabo. Project for the Palace of the Soviets, 1931. Plan and section.*

93. *Yamasaki, Hellmuth, and Leinweber. Air Terminal, St. Louis, Missouri, 1954. Interior.*

94. *Eero with T.W.A. model and staff.*

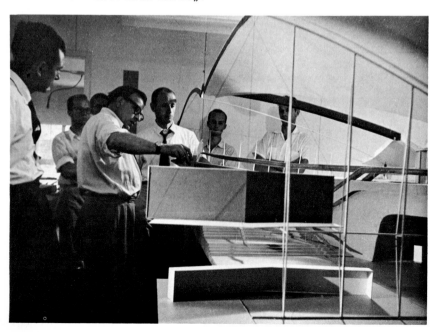

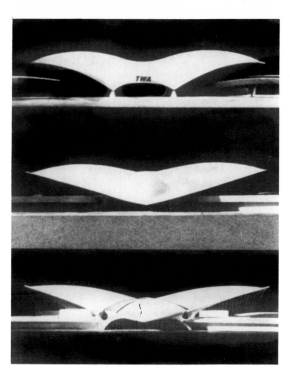

95. *T.W.A. Terminal. Models for first, second, and final structural concepts.*

96A. *T.W.A. Terminal, Idlewild Airport, 1956–62. Photo of front support, model.*

96B. *T.W.A. Terminal. Drawing developed from front support.*

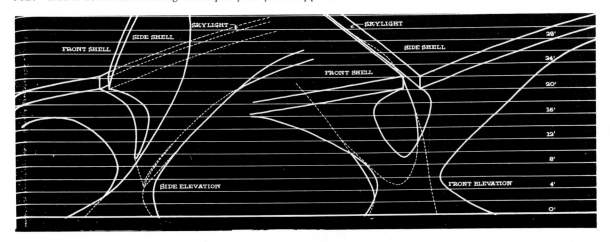

97. *T.W.A Terminal. Under construction. Exterior.*

98. *T.W.A. Terminal. Interior. (Photo: Ezra Stoller)*

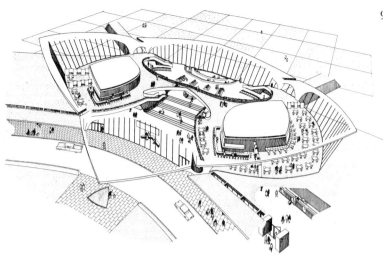

99. *T.W.A. Terminal. Cut-away drawing.*

100. *T.W.A. Terminal. Under construction.*
General view.

101. *T.W.A. Terminal. Interior.*
(Photo: Ezra Stoller)

102. *T.W.A. Terminal. Under construction. Exterior. (Photo: Ezra Stoller)*

103. *Dulles International Airport, Washington, D. C. Under construction, 1962.*

104. *Dulles Airport. Under construction.*

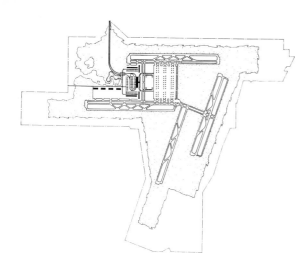

105. *Dulles Airport. Site plan.*

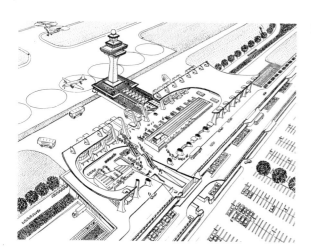

106. *Dulles Airport. Cut-away drawing.*

107A. *Dulles Airport. Plan.*

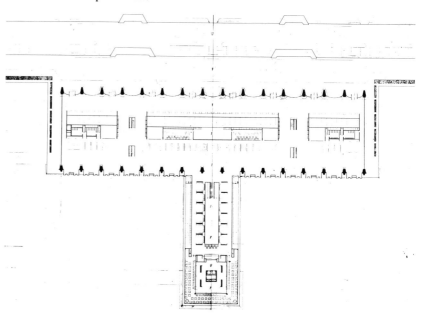

108. *Dulles Airport. Model with mobile lounges.*

109. *Dulles Airport. Mobile Lounge.*

107B. *Dulles Airport. Section.*

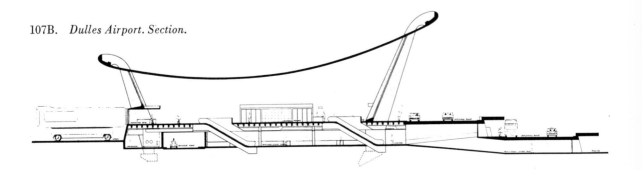

110. *Karl Gotthard Langhans. Brandenburg Gate, Berlin, 1799.*

111. *Le Corbusier. Chapel of Notre-Dame-du-Haut, Ronchamp, 1950–55.*

112. *Eric Mendelsohn. Imaginary drawing, 1917.*

113. *Dulles Airport. Under construction.*

114. *Dulles Airport. Under construction.*

115. *Dulles Airport. Under construction.*

116. *Women's Dormitory, University of Pennsylvania,*
      Philadelphia, Pennsylvania, 1957–60.

117. *Women's Dormitory, University of Pennsylvania. Interior court.*

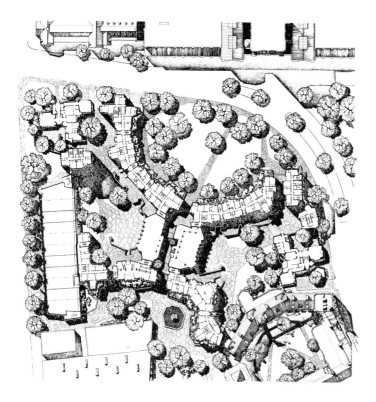

118. *Samuel F. B. Morse and Ezra Stiles Colleges, Yale University,*
New Haven, Connecticut. Site plan.

119. *Yale University Colleges. Under construction, 1962.*

120. *Yale University Colleges.*

121. *Vivian Beaumont Theater, Lincoln Center for the
Performing Arts, New York. Under construction, 1962. Model.*

122. *Vivian Beaumont Theater. Interior. Model.*

123. *World Health Organization, 1959, project. Model.*

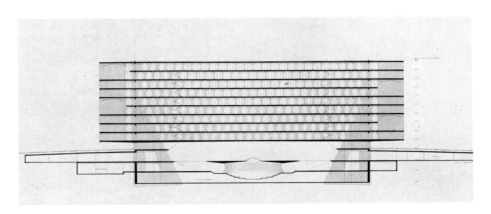

124A. *W.H.O. Structural section.*

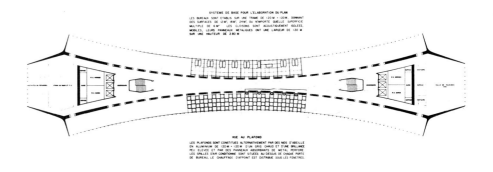

124B. *W.H.O. Upper-floor plan.*

125.   *Columbia Broadcasting System Headquarters Building, New York. Model. (Photo: Ezra Stoller)*

126. *Mies van der Rohe. Seagram Building, New York, 1958. (Photo: Ezra Stoller)*

127. *Nervi, Ponti, and Rosselli. Pirelli Building, Milan, 1955–59.*

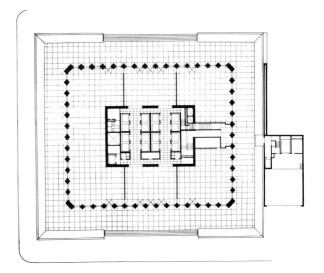

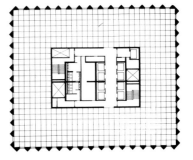

128. *C.B.S. Ground plan and office floor plan.*

129. *Jefferson Westward Expansion Memorial, St. Louis, Missouri, 1948. Competition rendering.*

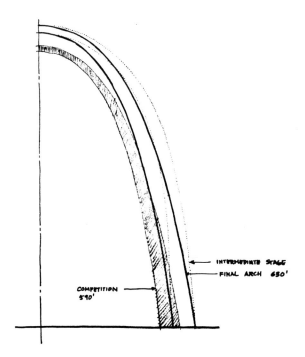

INTERMEDIATE STAGE
FINAL ARCH 630'

COMPETITION
590'

130. *Jefferson Memorial. Composite drawing.*

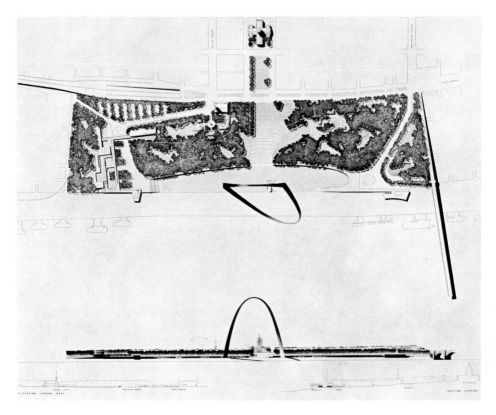

131. *Jefferson Memorial. Original (competition) site plan.*

132. *Jefferson Memorial, 1958. Final site plan.*

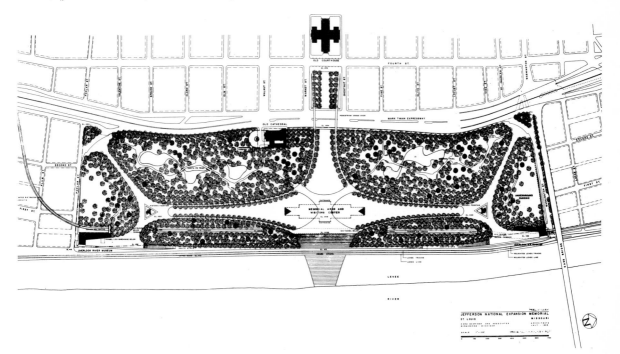

133.   *Jefferson Memorial. Model, final version.*

134.   *Jefferson Memorial. Model, final version.*

Fulfillment and Further Search

"The monument is a declaration of love and admiration to the higher purposes men hold in common."

LEWIS MUMFORD

Almost two miles away across the green Virginia countryside the great building comes into view with classic lucidity, massed in white splendor on its monumental base, its giant columns rising like muscular arms to hold aloft the long brow of the roof; and one knows instantly that this is the fulfillment of the search.

The road to this airport began not in Washington, twenty miles to the northeast, but goes back half a century in time and half around the world in space to a Finland still partly medieval, where a child was taught that truly civilized life means a total commitment to excellence, and that there is no final excellence without love. For this building is an unfettered act of the heart, strengthened by will, defined by intellect, but so lovingly shaped that as it is lost from sight, and appears again, still unexpectedly light and finely boned, but larger now, and still larger as the approach road bends past the lake—another Saarinen lake—and runs parallel to the façade lifting two hundred yards away, the immense form seems timeless. This is a Platonic ideal of an airport, imbued with Aristotelian realism, which the Masters of Chartres and Michelangelo might have fashioned, had such artists lived in the second half of the 20th century (plate 103).

The Washington International Airport, at Chantilly, Virginia —which by some strange historical paradox has been named for John Foster Dulles—is one of those rare symbols which proclaim the fundamental unities of an innovating age. Deeply personal though it was in conception, the airport is nevertheless an epochal monument in spirit and function, expressing and serving basic needs and aspirations of contemporary man, and thus transcending personal architecture. Even Hagia Sophia, one sometimes forgets, was designed by individuals celebrated in their time, but the name of the architect of this airport, like that of Isidore of Miletus, is secondary: what will matter to the future is that he was a 20th-century man.

And as one arrives on the high pedestal—a ceremonial platform as well as a functional utility—the monument, powerfully gaining scale, displays its full magnitude. One

114 after the other, down the 600-foot length of the façade, the great columns reach up sixty-five feet—in a massive gesture of sculptural freedom—through the curving sheet of the roof, to catch its upward flung edge at the height of its rise, and dynamically cast it backward, like a tremendous unraveled scroll, to be caught again as it streams upward to the lower colonnade in the rear. The entire structure acts and reacts in powerful, rhythmic consistency, welcoming, elevating the individual, rather than crushing him, with its broad, sheltering strength (plate 104).

For this building is made for man. Every detail—doors, canopies, balustrades—is scaled for humans, as in a Gothic cathedral, so that the impression of size is continually reinforced by visual reference between them and the grand elements of the composition: the low entrance between two columns, for example, is a measure of their grandeur. But more than this, the entire design is based on recognition of the functional as well as the emotional needs of man: this is one large airport—the terminal at Brasilia is perhaps the only other—where the traveler is humanely considered from his arrival to departure.

Here, as at General Motors and Bell Laboratories, Saarinen was dealing with a prototypical problem of Modern architecture on a new scale—for this is the first airport intended exclusively for jets (and possibly one day for conversion to rockets)—and he was compelled to interpret the nature of the air terminal from a completely new vantage point. Like most men who habitually travel by air, Saarinen was irritated by the enormous distances passengers had to walk through interminable corridors of a conventional finger-plan, which American architects senselessly repeated even though it had become increasingly unworkable. In some recent terminals, such as O'Hare Field in Chicago, different airline pavilions may be nearly a mile apart.

A radically different system of passenger handling was called for, and Saarinen found its germ in the buses used at some European fields to convey travelers from distant runways to the terminals. He reasoned that something more than an ordinary bus would be required, especially in a nation so technologically advanced as the United States, for to "add a bus to the process of getting from the ticket counter to the plane is a negative thing." He wanted a conveyance that would be positively luxurious, and then, as he studied the problem with expert associates, Ammann & Whitney, Burns & McDonnell, and Charles Landrum, it occurred to them that the problem could be solved simply "by combining the departure lounge and the moving vehicle into a single convenience, and by combining *that* with a covered gangplank which hitches directly to the plane." This meant that fingers could be omitted and that all the airlines could be housed in a single main structure, a union terminal, and also that the jets could remain far out in a "service station" area, close to runways, which are more simply organized than at any other field of this class (plates105–107).

Thus was born the idea of the already famous "mobile lounge": a major breakthrough in jetport design which will probably influence air facilities throughout the world. Built according to the crude notions of Chrysler's engineers, the mobile lounge is much less elegant than in Saarinen's proposed design—it has become a pugnaciously ugly monster of a vehicle—but it made possible an airport of consummate grace and efficiency through which passengers and baggage pass in easy, logical flow on two levels, across the short width of the long, narrow structure (plates 108, 109).

As soon as the mobile lounge proved feasible, the rest of the program lent itself admirably to Saarinen's vision of a linear terminal which could be extended in either direction, when necessary, to accommodate sixty or ninety gates without essentially altering the original thirty-six gate form. Because the site is a plain, Saarinen thought of the building as a low, hovering mass—"something between earth and sky"—but it could not be an inert mass: it must express its essential "spirit" and be "all one thing." Yet here was another complex problem: this building erected by the government of the United States, and serving many commercial airlines, by its nature would be several things. As an airport, Saarinen felt, its quality should be "nonstatic," but the structure was to be simultaneously a formal entrance to the American republic, or at least a gateway to its capital. Yet Federal architectural tradition is neo-Roman and static, even though the democratic ethos is not. Then again, this was not to be merely a national monument, but in the best sense a world facility belonging to an unprecedented age of travel—travel swifter than the speed of the day—and as such it symbolized the future.

The contending of these diverse motives, each still alive in the monument but magnificently fused in a single symbolic image, is the key to this design's greatness. This is one of the first truly convincing victories of the new architecture in its

116   quest—too often, a perversely unconfident quest—for a legitimate monumentalism worthy of a technological age. To see how far the world has come from the pseudo-monumentality that has ruled most official architecture for more than a century, it is necessary only to compare this gateway—vital with meanings for its own time—with a stillborn neo-classical pastiche such as the Brandenburg Gate in Berlin (plate 110). Only Le Corbusier at Chandigarh has gone so far—or further —in the same direction, and it is fascinating to find that Saarinen, when first contemplating the problem of capping his long, low structure, thought of a curved roof comparable to that of Ronchamp (plate 111).

Encouraged by his experience at the Yale rink, however, he turned to a suspension *parti*. He was not deterred by the engineering truth that a hung roof makes best sense in a circular structure, where its maximum efficiency is brought into play. Nor was he intimidated by the fact that the supporting pylons would have to be extremely heavy to take the load placed on them; he wished them even heavier, overstructured for the sake of overexpression, for he meant to contrast the weightlessness—that is, apparent weightlessness —of the roof with the massiveness of the understructure. The roof, lightly flying over an airy void, would be a sublimation of the forces working upward through the monument; and, following this subjective logic, he made the roof lower in back, to shelter incoming passengers, and higher in front, for monumental presence. This greatly intensified the spatial experience beneath it, but it taxed the structure correspondingly (plates 113, 114).

Thanks to Ammann & Whitney, particularly the firm's able chief structural designer Boyd Anderson, a covering of extreme lightness was devised (without relying, as at Yale, on so doubtful a material as wood). Precast concrete slabs were laid on the cables, and then grouted together to form a homogeneous membrane, which is a *chef-d'oeuvre* of engineered sculpture (plate 115).

The whole project—the whole fifteen square miles of the airport, whose borders, like G.M.'s, have been planted with a small forest of trees—is one of the great works of its time. If too many of Saarinen's earlier buildings suffered from lack of his personal attention, nothing now escaped the master's hand. Working with beautiful models which filled whole drafting rooms, he and his gifted staff, most notably Kevin Roche, deliberately, painstakingly, perfected the design. The proportions of the great base, the rightness of the immense superstructure, the virile upright of the control tower—the most powerful vertical form either Saarinen, father or son, ever used to contrast with a horizontal volume—all show Saarinen in complete control of his art. So, too, does every detail. The bush-hammered texture of the dignified limestone aggregate is a remarkable contribution to the Federal tradition of masonry building, and it has been sculpted with manly freedom. There is a consistent imaginative splendor in every canopy, every coping, every jamb, and—most splendid of all perhaps—in the curving extremities of the podium, carving their way through molded earthforms, and incomparably stronger than the same motive tried on a much smaller scale at the Yale rink.

But the crowning glory of this building is its space. This dynamic volume, swelling upward front and back, and flowing outward through the ends of the huge room, moving everywhere, but everywhere controlled (even, it would seem, beyond the building on the great expanse of the landing field and roads and lawns, and the happy lake: everywhere Saarinen's space, as Wright, Mies and Le Corbusier have had their unique space)—all this is a major stopping point of 20th-century art from which, as Saarinen wished, one moves on elated and enriched.

Saarinen was moving forward with absolute confidence and forthright daring. If his campus designs of the fifties had been only partly successful, and occasionally failures, and if a grimly muddled exterior could still invalidate the ambitious interior court of his University of Pennsylvania's women's dormitory (plates 116, 117), he returned to Yale to do two colleges which show the profession, once and for all, that a Modern architect may build honestly within the historical discipline of an existing neo-Gothic environment. The undisguised medievalism of the design, in which towers, courts, twisting passages, refectories, dormitories, and master's lodges are crowded on a site flanked by the great piles of the Payne Whitney gymnasium and the Graduate School, elicited Paul Rudolph's remark that Saarinen had created "a stage setting for Ivanhoe" (plates 118–120). Saarinen smiled, but he knew well what he was doing. This part of the Yale campus was not the place to desert a masonry idiom. In the New Haven adaptation of the Oxford system, the residential colleges are little educational communities in themselves, with their butteries for drinking and libraries for reading. Saari-

118 nen regarded them as justifiably artificial "monasteries" in the midst of a chaotic world from which young people might well be momentarily sheltered.

His intention was to achieve a comparable atmosphere without resorting to handicraft stonework. After considerable research, he and associate John Dinkeloo adapted and improved a Norwegian process which enabled them to build a "technological masonry wall" by filling forms with rough stones, injecting concrete grout under high pressure, and later troweling out the excess mortar. With this material he constructed robustly irregular buildings, closely related in mass and modeling and color to the older structures around them, and sharing their virtues, such as a wonderful variety of accommodations in which no two rooms are the same. Saarinen hoped this technological stone wall might have wide application, but the invention, charming as it is, surely has less importance than does the environmental principle of the total design of the Yale colleges. The Yale campus can be recognized today as a fine and permanent cityscape, only superficially romantic; and if so dauntless a Modern designer could subject his art to such surroundings, for the sake of the whole, there is yet hope for urban continuity in this country.

Saarinen was also working in the most thoroughly urban environment America has to offer: Manhattan. In company with Gordon Bunshaft—one of the few contemporaries whose architecture he valued and with whom he had long collaborated as a penetrating critic-consultant for Skidmore, Owings & Merrill's Air Academy—he was designing the Vivian Beaumont Theater for Lincoln Center. (Saarinen, with Jo Mielziner as another co-designer, was doing the theater interior, and Bunshaft the adjoining library-museum; but the two architects shared responsibility for the exterior and the over-all structural concept.) Together they produced a vigorously boned concrete structure in which there is not the slightest evidence of a clash of wills, and which should be by far the strongest and most direct building in the nest of neo-façadism that the "cultural supermarket" of Lincoln Center is likely to become (plate 121). The auditorium within is all Saarinen and Mielziner, and promises to be a triumph of flexible planning, with its vast (11,000 square foot) stage which can be adapted quickly to any condition a repertory company may require, as well as perfect visibility and acoustics (plate 122).

The theater will be overshadowed by one of Saarinen's

last, and certainly one of his greatest, commissions: the 38-story tower for the Columbia Broadcasting System that will rise on the Avenue of the Americas between 52nd and 53rd Streets. The site, on the northwest edge of Rockefeller Center, confronts a collection of grossly undistinguished, recent skyscrapers, with more to come in the vicinity. Yet it is not these elephantine neighbors, but Mies van der Rohe's Seagram Building across town on Park Avenue, with which C.B.S. will inevitably be compared. Seagram probably will remain the culminating masterpiece of skeletal towers of metal and glass. It is difficult to conceive of a tall building more masterfully ordered. Nearby Lever House, a fair building in its own right, is crushed by Seagram's bronze sobriety, for Mies' objective passion (which in his architecture is not a contradiction of terms) and his grave intelligence make even outstanding new buildings appear strident and thin (plate 126).

Saarinen sought a radically different, but equally uncompromising purism in C.B.S.: he wished it to be "the simplest skyscraper statement in New York." Never before, it should be remembered, had Saarinen designed an important high-rise structure. Aside from the unexecuted, steel-framed office slab for General Motors, there was only the fantastic project in concrete for a nine-story headquarters for the World Health Organization near Geneva (plates 123, 124), which took second place in an international competition in 1959. The most arresting feature of this wildly sculptural design, beyond its unique articulation of differing functional spaces in plan and elevation, would have been the diminishing mass of its central structure. Toward either end of the building, huge, paired triangular supports were to lift the glazed slab free of the ground, and angle upward to the roof. Strung between these gigantic members, like curving lattices, were twin diagonal grids, which in plan arched inward beside an asymptotic central axis, and which grew lighter as they ascended. The prime office space on the cantilevered floors would have been column-free; the façades, equally unencumbered by structure, would have been transparent.

The W.H.O. design was anything but simple, but it deserves comparison with more objective concrete structures of the late fifties, including the Pirelli Building at Milan, for which Pier Luigi Nervi devised four massive, tapering pylons that ascend thirty stories. Although Pirelli was weakened by architect Gio Ponti's vulgar execution, Nervi's structural concept is a classic expression of the handling of forces in a tower of reinforced concrete. Yet like the Miesian cage of metal, Pirelli is a "skin-and-bones" building: its structural bones are merely bigger and fewer and plastic; the skin remains glass (plate 127).

Although, characteristic of this late period, Saarinen adopted a concrete structural *parti* for C.B.S., "skin-and-bones" was precisely the idiom he was determined to renounce in a city rapidly filling up with glass buildings, most of them as bad as Seagram is good. Rather than as a transparent volume then, even though the interior is a structural void except for the floors and service core, he conceived C.B.S. as a mass: a solid-appearing shaft, enclosed by narrowly separated, triangular columns clad in dark granite, with intervening windows of matching dark glass that will appear as a heavy film between the tremendous, unchanging uprights: "a proud and soaring thing" (plate 125). The ringing phrase is of course Louis Sullivan's, but only in this sense is C.B.S. "Sullivanesque"—as it has been mistakenly described. Whatever Sullivan's "organic" architecture was, it was far from simplistic. In spite of its over-all assenting grace, a Sullivan tower, like a classical column, was inevitably composed of clearly differentiated parts: a base, shaft, and top; and it met both sky and ground with decisive finality.

Saarinen's tower, soaring out of a sunken plaza, with no architectural identification of the meager entrances on the side streets, and no entrance whatever on the narrow side it turns to the broad avenue, has no base at all. It leaps straight out of the ground, ascending the full thirty-eight stories without a break in profile, but eventually shoots into the sky.

Granted, this is simplicity. But one may also ask if it is not oversimplification. Rationally a tower—especially a masonry tower—should throw off weight as it ascends, as in fact this tower does internally. Yet the diminution of mass is confined to the interior, and is not even clearly expressed there. From the nineteenth floor upward the columns are hollowed out to contain air-conditioning ducts. Thus C.B.S., unlike Pirelli, does not grow *visually* more open and light as it rises; and it would seem that the architect missed a wonderful opportunity to make a truly new statement of simplicity in concrete, which could have remained as subjectively strong—or stronger —than the statement he actually made.

A great deal was missed in this design, however, at least partly because C.B.S. decided on a more modest program than

Seagram. There is, to be sure, a plaza; but it is scarcely more than a protective border for the freestanding tower, and is in no sense a real civic space. Saarinen recognized this by sinking its surface below street level, in a rare exception to his usual policy of elevating a monument on a pedestal. Although this building, rising like a gigantic granite stele, cannot escape monumentality, some of the indispensable necessities of monumental grandeur have been omitted. The insistence of C.B.S. that commercial premises be included on the ground floor, for example, accounts for the small lobbies that will always be lighted artificially; yet there must have been some better solution to the problem of the tiny entrances, just as there must have been a better alternative to the ungainly corner of the building, which logically requires an angle, but instead is faced with the broad plane of a doubled column, as if the modular plan somehow had not worked out correctly (plate 128).

In time, Saarinen surely, indomitably, would have worked out the problem of the skyscraper, just as he did the problem of the airport. When one considers that C.B.S. might have stood in relation to a later tower in the way that T.W.A. precedes the masterpiece at Washington, or that General Motors precedes Bell, or the Chicago Law School the Yale Colleges, then the loss of this fearless architect, searching where others did not care to search, finding where they did not dream of discovery, appears in its full tragedy as one of the cultural disasters of modern times.

Modern mass society demands masters, as if they were automatically manufactured by egalitarianism, but the poignant fact remains, in spite of the puffs of *Time* and the architectural press: they are few in any age, and too often crushed by the unprecedented pressures of the present, which must build more intelligently and humanely than any previous age if the world itself is to be truly civilized. The master architect, like all great artists, must have that prolonged inner fortitude, which Saarinen and his father as Finns called *sisu:* the kind of moral strength which kept a runner such as Paavo Nurmi running when he was theoretically spent.

Saarinen was never spent, but was struck down at the height of the race, still in the forefront, striding confidently, when he was seized, without the slightest warning, by brain cancer in August, 1961. Two weeks later he was dead. Had he been given another dozen years, in view of what he had accomplished in the dozen preceding, from the time he won the Jefferson competition in 1948, the results for world architecture—and indeed for the world—would have been incalculable. He was helping to create not merely a new order of architecture, but a new order of man: the man of the future for whom the great arch of steel is at last being built beside the Mississippi.

The history of the Jefferson Memorial reveals Saarinen's perfectionism at its searching best. In the decade that he waited for the railroad to be relocated from the levee to a tunnel back from the riverfront, so that the monument and its surrounding park could be built without an unsightly blemish, he studied and restudied the design. As the work went ahead in 1958, he drew upon his experience with curving forms at M.I.T., the Yale rink, and T.W.A., seeking a faultless arch form, contemplating the monumental arches of the past, and the vaults and buttresses of Gothic cathedrals, reflecting on the energy that a curved line develops in space, and on the paradox of its downward direction.

He wished this arch to rise up in a single aspiring movement. He built models, and rebuilt them, studying them with mirrors, photographing them, and rebuilding them again, heightening the arch from the original 590 to 630 feet, then drawing its profile inward in a further refinement, until he arrived at the magnificent final form (plates 129–132). At the same time he worked with the engineers—Severud's firm —and the inner triangular frame of structural steel and its radiant sheathing of stainless steel were also refined. He talked with inventors about the little vehicles which will carry visitors upward inside the soaring hoop, through a dark triangular tunnel, to the tremendous vision of the heartland of America that opens from the observation bubble at the top.

It was all coming together now, becoming one thing, taking its place between earth and sky. The rather dry original site plan was enriched with surging baroque vigor: the curve of the arch was repeated, and repeated again, in paths and walls, and suggested in water. In a single lordly gesture Saarinen cast one of the great staircases of the world across the width of the riverfront, descending in broad steps to the bank on which Lewis and Clark debarked. The arch itself was moved to a rise of ground, farther from the river, closer to the city; and the terrain again was sculpted, molded, shaped, reshaped; and when Saarinen had the land as he wished, he knew that it should be planted with a small forest of trees (plates 133–134).

In the trees there was a memory of the woods at "Hvitträsk," but they were also a symbol of the American wilderness into which explorers had forged. The clearing from which the arch would rise, in single magnificence, was the image of the primitive clearings in which they had camped, while the great Virginian—our only architect President—wished them westward, ever westward, carrying forward the destiny of the nation and the world, and this selfless spirit of discovery, by men for other men, is what the monument should commemorate forever.

Chronology

1910   Born August 20, Kirkkonummi, Finland

1922   Father wins second prize Chicago *Tribune* competition

1923   Arrives in United States

1925   Family settles at Cranbrook

1929–30   Studies sculpture at Paris

1930–34   Yale School of Architecture

1934–36   Travel in Europe

1936   Joins father's firm and Cranbrook faculty

1939   Marries Lily Swann (divorced 1953)
Wins Smithsonian competition

1940   With Charles Eames wins two first prizes for furniture design, Museum of Modern Art

1942–45   Duty with the Office of Strategic Services

1948   Wins Jefferson Memorial competition

1950   Death of his father

1953   Marries Aline B. Louchheim

1956   Wins London Embassy competition

1960   Elected Fellow, American Academy of Arts and Letters

1961   Dies September 1, at Ann Arbor, after brain surgery

1962   Posthumously awarded Gold Medal, American Institute of Architects

Selected Bibliography

(Abbreviations: *Architectural Forum—AF; Architectural Record—AR; Progressive Architecture—PA.*)

By Eero Saarinen

"Campus Planning: The Unique World of the University," *AR*, November 1960.
"Changing Philosophy of Architecture," *AR*, August 1954.
"Function, Structure and Beauty," *Architectural Association Journal*, July–August 1957.
"Six Broad Currents of Modern Architecture," *AF*, July 1953.
Statements on several buildings in "Recent Work of Eero Saarinen," *Zodiac #4* (1959). Excellent coverage of Jefferson, Yale Rink, T.W.A., I.B.M., Rochester, and late furniture.

On Eero Saarinen

Carter, Peter. "Eero Saarinen, 1910–1961," *Architectural Design* (London), December 1961.
Haskell, Douglas. "Eero Saarinen, 1910–1961," *AF*, October 1961.
Lessing, Lawrence. "The Diversity of Eero Saarinen," *AF*, July 1960.
Louchheim, Aline B. (later Mrs. Eero Saarinen). "Now Saarinen the Son," *New York Times Magazine*, April 26, 1953.
McQuade, Walter. "Eero Saarinen, a Complete Architect," *AF*, April 1962.
Temko, Allan. "Eero Saarinen: Something between Earth and Sky," an interview, *Horizon*, July 1960.
Time, profile entitled, "The Maturing Modern," July 2, 1956.
Two books by Eliel Saarinen, *The City: Its Growth—Its Decay—Its Future* (New York: Reinhold, 1943) and *Search for Form* (Reinhold, 1948), should be consulted as expressions of his father's philosophy.
   Albert Christ-Janer's biography, *Eliel Saarinen* (University of Chicago Press, 1948), contains important material on Eero's childhood and early career, although it undervalues his contribution to certain joint projects, such as the design for the Smithsonian Gallery, on which he and his father collaborated.

On Individual Buildings and Projects

Bell Laboratories: *AF*, July 1960.
Columbia Broadcasting System Headquarters: *AF*, April 1962.
Concordia Senior College: *PA*, December 1958.
Crow Island School: *AF*, August 1941.
Deere & Co.: *AF*, July 1960.
Detroit, project for Civic Center: *AF*, April 1949.
Drake University: Campus Plan, *AR*, December 1947;; Science and Pharmacy Buildings, *PA*, November 1950; Dormitories and Dining Hall, *PA*, April 1955.
Furniture: "Eero Saarinen as Furniture Designer" by Peter Carter, *Architectural Design* (London), October 1957; "A Chair is a Chair is a Chair," *Architect's Journal* (London), August 22, 1957; *AF*, July 1957; *Zodiac #4*; "Designs for Living" by John Anderson, *Playboy*, July 1961.
General Motors Technical Center: comprehensive articles in *AF*, November 1954 and May 1956, as well as preliminary coverage in issue of July 1949 which shows projected slab tower. Earliest version of

design in Christ-Janer's *Eliel Saarinen*. See also *General Motors Engineering Journal*, May–June 1956, for interesting technical information.

I.B.M., Rochester, Minn.: *Zodiac #4* and *AF*, October 1958.

I.B.M., Yorktown, N.Y.: *AF*, June 1961, and *AR*, June 1961.

Irwin Union Bank & Trust Company, Columbus, Indiana: *AF*, October 1955. Article also discusses nearby Christ Church and general character of this architecturally adventurous small city.

Jefferson Westward Expansion Memorial: *Zodiac #4;* see also special supplements of St. Louis *Post-Dispatch*, January 19, 1958 and May 7, 1961.

Lincoln Center Repertory Theater: *AF*, April 1962; and *The Performing Arts*, newsletter published by Lincoln Center, November 14, 1961.

London Embassy: *AF*, March 1961, contains statements by British critics, some very harsh, and reply by Saarinen; see also *Architectural Review* (London), April 1961, and *The Architect and Building News* (London), December 7, 1960.

Milwaukee War Memorial: *Zodiac #4* and *AF*, December 1957.

M.I.T. Auditorium and Chapel: *AF*, July 1955, and especially issue of March 1956, which contains critiques by Bruno Zevi, J.M. Richards, and Sigfried Giedion (remarks attributed to Pier Luigi Nervi by Zevi were later denied by the great Italian engineer but were apparently accurately quoted) ; see also *Zodiac #4* and *Technology Review* (published by M.I.T.), July 1955.

Oslo Embassy: *AF* and *AR*, December 1959.

Residences: "A Contemporary Palladian Villa," *AF*, September 1958, a work significant not merely because of its classical presence and large-span interiors, but also because it clearly reveals the hand of Kevin Roche, then Saarinen's chief assistant, and now partner in charge of design of the firm, which continues as Eero Saarinen & Associates; home for John Entenza, designed by Eero Saarinen and Charles Eames, *AF*, September 1950; and project for "Unfolding House" shown with other early designs in *Monthly Bulletin, Michigan Society of Architects*, July 1953.

T.W.A., Idlewild: *AF*, January 1958, August 1960, and December 1960; and *AR*, September 1961.

University of Chicago Law School, Dormitory, and Dining Hall: *AR*, November 1960.

University of Michigan, North Campus Plan: *AF*, June 1953.

University of Pennsylvania, Dormitory: *AF*, February 1961; and *The Pennsylvania Gazette* (published by the University), February 1961, in which Saarinen explains his concept in an interview.

Vassar College, Dormitory: *AR*, September 1959.

Washington International Airport: *AF*, July 1960, May and September 1961, and April 1962; *AR*, March 1960; and for general background of the project, "The Birth of an Airport" by Walter McQuade, *Fortune*, March 1962.

World Health Organization Headquarters, competition entry: *Architecture d'Aujourd'hui* (Paris), April 1960.

Yale University, Hockey Rink: *AF*, December 1958; *AR*, August 1957 and October 1958; and *Zodiac #4*.

Yale University, Residence Colleges: *AF*, July 1960 and April 1962; *AR*, February 1960; and *Yale News*, special supplement, November 12, 1959.

Index

Numbers in regular roman type refer to text pages; *italic* figures refer to the plates.